Tsunami 2004
Unawatuna, Sri Lanka

TRACEY LEE

DEDICATION

For Luke Lloyd Warren, my partner and my best friend, who is always there
by my side to make everything alright.

In memory of all those who lost their lives on 26th December 2004

ACKNOWLEDGEMENTS

Heartfelt thanks to Pat and Fran Warren for initially pushing me to write this book when we returned from Sri Lanka; Lucy Popescu for reading the beginning for advising me to 'keep going' and then, later, for editing the manuscript; my old chum, Abigail McGarry, for telling me to write an account about the Tsunami even just for friends to read; Nicky Blundred who read and corrected an early draft time and time again – she said she didn't mind, but I'm not so sure; Avril, my mum, and Dawn, my little sis, who had to relive the tsunami nightmare all over again by writing down their responses. I know this was very painful for you both but thank you, I love you.

Finally, to Andy James, our friend, who relayed the message that we were alive to my family.

Thank you to all our friends who shared tears with us as we tried to digest the horrors that unfolded and who supported me while I locked myself away to write this book. You all listened patiently as I repeated the story over and over again and stopped me going mad.

Thank you to Jackie and Jim, Dale and Nick, Dawn and Rob, Laura and Nick, Amanda and Fergus, Alan and Andrea, Malcolm and Tanya, Laura and Dean, Lil Ju, Vanessa and Gerald, Kirsteen and Nick, I love you all.

Many thanks to all my colleagues and friends at London Zoo who supported me at work when I was low and made me laugh – there are too many to mention but you know who you are.

Luke, who is my best friend, my love, my rock, thanks for your support, I love you.

And of course Thalik, our friend from Zimmer Rest, Unawatuna, an amazing person – many thanks for everything you did to help us.

This book was edited by Lucy Popescu.

A massive thank you to my friend Dylan Costello for helping me get my book into print.

PREFACE

Boxing Day, 2004, in Sri Lanka was a day when many people lost their lives in a 'freak act of nature'. Asia experienced the second largest earthquake on record in the Indian Ocean, off the west coast of Sumatra, releasing massive tsunamis which brought death and devastation throughout the region. The mega-thrust earthquake created a geological catastrophe and approximately six hundred miles of fault lines ruptured in the Asian sea. Two of the planet's plates went head to head. As one pushed down on the other it was squeezed and the pressure built up until the plates erupted, releasing an enormous amount of energy. The sea bed rose and within seconds the water column shifted to create a massive wall of water.

The tsunami started to travel in different directions across the Indian basin. Although this was picked up by experts at the Pacific Tsunami Warning Centre in Honolulu, there was no warning system in place in Asia. This meant there was no time for people to evacuate the beaches and head inland. Had a system been in place this would be a very different story and many unnecessary deaths could have been prevented.

Early that morning, everyone was blissfully unaware of the horrors that lay ahead. They were going about their daily chores, eating their breakfast, taking a dip in the crystal water or lying on the beach catching the early morning sun rays, happy and relaxed. What began as a normal day for hundreds of thousands of people turned out to be one of the most catastrophic days in history.

In Sri Lanka alone, somewhere between thirty-eight thousand and thirty-nine thousand people became victims of the tsunami. It is estimated that at least three hundred thousand people died in twelve different countries throughout Asia and Africa on that day – the exact figure may never be known. The countries affected were Sri Lanka, Indonesia, India, Thailand, the Maldives, the Seychelles, Bangladesh, Burma, Kenya, Malaysia, Somalia and Tanzania.

I started to write down my account of the tsunami on my return to England to try and help me come to terms with what happened in Sri Lanka on Boxing Day. I hoped it would help me to understand what I had witnessed and make some sense of this terrible tragedy. It was cathartic writing about my experiences so I just kept going. I soon realised that there was masses to write about, so as the weeks turned into months, my notes turned into a book. By writing down my account I found some peace.

It all seems a million miles away and somewhat surreal, sitting here in London in front of my computer on my return. The sky is grey and low, and it's about to snow. The winter light is casting its magical brightness against the leafless trees. People are walking past my window all wrapped up in thick scarves and hats, with hunched shoulders, looking gloomy on their way to work. The Christmas festivities are over. The recycling boxes in the front gardens are overflowing with wine bottles, boxes and Christmas paper. Christmas trees stand in window bays with drooping branches and flickering lights.

I sit and think about the tsunami, about how precious and fragile life is. I have been given a second chance. I now feel death is always close by, but I intend to enjoy every precious moment I have left, to honour the memory of those who were so cruelly taken.

This book is dedicated to all those who lost their lives in the tsunami on 26 December 2004 and to the beautiful Sri Lankan people, who looked after us despite losing everything they owned and loved. Their kindness and generosity will never be forgotten and I am eternally grateful. I thank you from the bottom of my heart.

You have two choices after surviving: One is to become a victim; the other is to become a survivor.

CHAPTERS

1 - PROLOGUE

As I lay in the Whittington Hospital Labour Ward in north London on 26 December 2009, exhausted and traumatised my hormones all at sea, my mind began to wander. The room was dark with a winter sky outside. I lay and listened in my deathly quiet room to the screams and animal like howling of women in labour. It sounded like they were being murdered as their contractions ripped through their bodies.

A tear rolled down my face and headed off towards my ear and onto the pillow. I looked out of the window of this old Victorian hospital. Its sinister looking architecture was silhouetted against the moonlight and the orange glow from the street lights reminded me of a stage set for a horror film. It made the screaming even more eerie and a shiver ran down my spine as I wrapped the sheet around me to comfort myself. I could hear the hum of the double decker buses, climbing Highgate Hill, taking people home after their Boxing Day shenanigans.

I remembered five years to the day, Boxing Day 2004, and the screams of a mother as she searched for her baby and the shrieks of utter despair as she held her baby close to her chest, his limp little body in her arms, his pale legs dangling. His name was Harry.

Tonight, here in London, I finally understood what Harry's mum had felt. I had been a mum only for a short time, I had never had the chance to hold, kiss, cuddle or feed him. I hadn't had the opportunity to laugh with delight as he chuckled or look deep into his eyes as he looked back at me because our baby had been born sleeping.

There was now some sort of understanding, a connection with this woman, a stranger. I had witnessed her raw grief, the helpless look in her eyes as she held her dead baby boy in her arms. She had known Harry for six months of his short life. She had held and kissed him, loved and cherished him, fed and cuddled him and in a second she had lost him.

The screams of the women in the labour ward made my blood run cold and transported me back to that day, the screams of people fighting for their lives in the dirty water as their loved ones were swept to their deaths. Boxing Day, 2004, Sri Lanka; I still remember the tsunami with great fear. I thought of Harry and as I lay and cried for the loss of my own baby boy, I also wept for him and his mummy.

Throughout the night, I drifted in and out of sleep with Luke sitting next to me holding my hand. We had our own room away from the new mothers and their celebrations. It was sterile and empty with a purple flower on the card on the door to let the midwives changing shifts know we were 'that couple'.

I watched the Christmas tinsel shimmer in the heat from the old radiator and listened to two midwives outside the room chatting about their Christmas, laughing and gossiping. Everything felt surreal. Sometimes a murderous scream stopped...silence...then the cries of a new born baby could be heard.

I imagined baby Harry being born and his parents' joy and wondered what it felt like to hold your own living, breathing baby in your arms, for it was something I was not going to experience this cold Boxing Day night.

Another tear ran from the corner of my eye followed by many more.

2 – HOLIDAY IN SRI LANKA, 2004

My father-in-law, Patrick Warren, or Pat as we affectionately know him, grew up in Ceylon with his older brother Robert. Their parents, both Irish born and bred, managed a tea plantation situated in Kegalle, about thirty miles from the royal city of Kandy, the hill country capital. The plantation was called Gollinda. Pat's father had moved there after the war as he loved the tropical climate and way of life in Ceylon.

The family lived in the rolling hills among the tea plantations until Pat and Robert were teenagers. Their mother had never really taken to living in the country and was very lonely. She drank and smoked heavily. At the age of fourteen, Pat was sent to England with Robert, to get an English education. It was a massive upheaval for two young lads – to leave their parents and the country that was their home.

After a sea voyage that lasted weeks the boys were met by their Aunt Vivienne, who they hardly knew, and were taken to their new boarding school. Alone and vulnerable they struggled to adjust to their new environment, missing their parents and friends terribly. In the following years they went back to Ceylon only twice during the school holidays before their mother died.

Pat grew up to be a kind and generous man with unusual interests from ghost-hunting to Tai Chi. He met his wife Fran at Manchester University and together they had five children and created a warm family home in Wandsworth, South London. Pat lives life to the full, sculpting stone in his studio, teaching art, smoking fat cigars and driving a London Black Taxi. Fran is a professor of Art History at Kingston University and enjoys a busy career and a lively family life. Pat and Fran have travelled widely and have many fabulous tales to tell and words of wisdom. They visited Iran and Afghanistan in the 1970s and I love listening to their crazy stories. The couple has taught Buddhism for more than twenty years. They are both practicing Buddhists and every Monday the sound of people chanting from their home fills the air in Wandsworth.

My partner, Dr Luke Warren, is Pat and Fran's eldest son. He is a former elephant keeper with a passion for animals. Luke enjoys travelling and big adventures. He now works in climate change. His other passion is his tropical garden and koi carp which he continually changes and develops. We have been together for twenty years.

I am the team leader of 'Mammals South' at London Zoo in Regents Park, where I manage fifteen keepers. This section has all the big cats, bears, pygmy hippos, apes and monkeys, gorillas and monkeys, camels and bearded pigs. I have worked at the zoo for twenty years and really love my job. It is challenging and very rewarding – no day is ever the same. I feel very lucky to do what I love.

With his children all grown up, Pat had decided to pursue his cherished dream of returning to his childhood home of Ceylon. Being a large family this was always going to be a difficult task due to everyone's busy schedules and the difficulty in synchronizing holidays from work. Pat set his heart on

Christmas 2004 and asked everyone to get the time off so that we could travel together.

Camille, Luke's younger sister, was training to be a barrister. She has strong protective feelings about our planet and strives to change things. Next in the family is Duncan, the joker of the family who, with a philosophy degree behind him, analyses life in an interesting way. At the time, he was teaching English in Japan. Nathan had just completed his degree and was taking a year off to travel. Last, but not least, is Saskia. She's blonde and slim with an infectious laugh. She was studying English and Art at Oxford. She wanted to follow in her mother's footsteps and become an art curator or something similar.

After months of preparation, the flights were booked for December 18th. We were embarking on an adventure to rediscover Pat's childhood and enjoy a family Christmas in the sunny tropics of Sri Lanka. I was counting down the days at work. Duncan was flying from Japan to meet us and Nathan was flying from Thailand. It was going to be a big reunion.

We arrived at Heathrow airport full of anticipation and pleased to be leaving cold, dark England for a few weeks. At the check-in desk we were shocked to be told that we would not be able to fly due to the airline overbooking its seats. Soon enough our politeness was replaced by anger. We demanded to talk to the manager. The staff told us to go home and that they hoped to get us on a plane in the next two to three days.

Any delay would lead to all kinds of complications as Duncan and Nathan were both meeting us in Colombo. We had no way of contacting them. My mother-in-law Fran, normally one of the most placid people I have ever known, turned into a raging bull. They wanted us to leave the check-in area but we refused. We were going nowhere until this was resolved. We watched the big clock on the wall until our take-off time had come and gone and demanded to see the manager again.

An imperious looking woman with a heavy frown marched across the concourse. She wore a dark blue suit and a hat with a veil, which floated behind her as she walked, her high heels clipped smartly as if to emphasise her importance. She was like a Queen Bee with her little helpers running, chattering, pointing at us, ensuring they got their version of events across to her first. We were furious and unleashed our anger on her. She replied, tersely, that it was common practice to overbook an aircraft. After remonstrating with her, she gave us sixty pounds worth of vouchers for the restaurant and told us she was going to try and get us on a plane.

Eventually she managed to get us onto another flight three hours later which was a relief. We were each £200 richer in compensation. All six of us piled onto one of those airport buggies. We looked ridiculous hanging on for dear life with the driver zipping along through the crowds moaning at how he would lose his job if his boss saw him.

The flight, I'm glad to say, was uneventful. The views from the window were breath taking at times, especially as we flew over the Maldives. The islands have the most astonishing coral reefs layered around them with fantastic shades of turquoise and blue seas encircling them – a sight that takes your breath away.

3 - COLOMBO

We arrived in Colombo the following day. I hate flying. As we came into land I closed my eyes and hummed, my palms were sweating. The loud buzzing of the landing gear opening and the thud as the wheels locked into place made me shudder. The bump as the plane's wheels hit the runway and the roaring of the engines as the pilot broke made me sigh with relief – we were on land. As we stepped off the plane, the sun was shining, heavy warm air greeted us, and the sound of crickets filled the air.

Fresh off the plane we were easy pickings. As soon as we walked towards the taxis various local men ran towards us, jabbering their fares. We started to barter with them for a fair price into the centre of Colombo, but Pat soon tired of this. He got wads of money out of his wallet and the men's eyes lit up. Pat asked how much they wanted to go to the centre.

"No, it's not the way Pat!" cried Saskia, "they will rip you off."

"Shush you lot," he said, and waved his hand at us to go away.

Pat just wanted to relax. He was a seasoned traveller, not a teenager on a budget. He hadn't got time for all this malarkey. I watched him, amused. Suddenly these men had no interest in dealing with us. Pat was the object of their desire and they swarmed around him, like vultures on a carcass, pulling at his top.

Eventually, laughing, we climbed into a bus. Nathan had nicknamed Pat 'ATM', telling him that he had acted like a cash machine handing out money left, right and centre. Pat comes from a different generation, one that considers it rude to argue and barter over pennies. For us lot, on our usual tight holiday budgets, it's the norm.

Sri Lanka is a vibrant, culturally diverse country of eighteen million people. The island has rolling hills, rainforests, windswept plains and beautiful beaches. Religion pervades many aspects of life. There are Buddhist and Hindu temples, as well as mosques and churches. Varying degrees of colonial impact, modernising influences, wealth and income add other shades to the cultural mosaic. The country is located at the crossroads where east meets west and is regarded as the gateway to south Asia. It is practically in the centre of the Indian Ocean and has climatic and cultural links with three countries. It is teeming with bird life and exotic animals and I couldn't wait to explore it.

We arrived at our guesthouse, Shrubbery Gardens, where Duncan was waiting for us. He was standing on the main balcony, waving, with a huge grin across his face. He had been starting to worry as we were behind schedule. It didn't seem like a year since I had last seen him— he looked just the same, his cheeky face full of mischief.

We were all laughing as we flopped into the old colonial chairs clumped together on the balcony. We ordered pots of tea which were served in the finest bone china tea cups. The warm heat massaged our winter-beaten skin. Birds were picking at the berries on the fruit trees, the flowers lining the road were orange and shocking pink, my favourite colours. It was beautiful.

To our delight, the guest house was clean and comfortable with white starched sheets on the beds. It was owned by Mrs Marie Barbara Settupathy, a no-nonsense kind of woman, heavyset but attractive, and dressed in western clothes. As we were so late, she had been suspicious of Duncan and had threatened to give our rooms away. She was obviously used to young travellers letting her down and costing her money so was very pleased when we arrived but she seemed to have taken a dislike to Duncan.

We had showers and freshened up before heading into town. I put on my cool, cotton skirt and a pink flowery top, lipstick, mascara, and a splash of Paloma Picasso. I combed my wet hair, popped my sunglasses on my head and slipped into my pink, sparkly flip flops. Finally I slathered myself in sun lotion before grabbing my pink wicker bag ready to fill with my purchases.

We set off to explore Colombo, the capital city and commercial centre of Sri Lanka. Pat already seemed very much at home as he ambled along the roads with a look of contentment on his face. I felt a mixture of joy and sadness, wondering what he might be feeling as he remembered his past.

It was like being in India. The heat, chaos, gem shops galore, the endless beeping of horns and the smell of delicious Asian cooking filled the air, disguising that familiar smell of eggy drains that you always get abroad. Colombo has many modern facilities and grand shopping malls. Well-off city folk, dressed in designer clothes and clutching shopping bags and mobile phones, rushed around while beggars with limbs missing and haunted faces lay in the gutter, day and night. The two extremes exist side-by-side.

Smiling men sold sweet coconuts by the roadside. They skillfully hacked off the tops with their machetes and poked straws through for us to drink the sweet milk inside. One coconut costs about one hundred and fifty rupees, which is about sixty pence at home. I wondered how they managed to make a living as every few metres there was another smiling man holding his machete.

Street vendors were frying little bowl-shaped pancakes over high flames with fried eggs in the middle of them. Pat explained that they were called egg hoppers and were delicious when eaten with a runny curry sauce. They smelled lovely so we all had one and they were divine!

Feeling the hectic clamour of city life, I couldn't wait to start shopping, which is Luke's worst nightmare.

He always asks me: "Why do you want that?" or, "Do you need it?" or, "How much have you spent?"

I lie, irritated by his questioning. "It was ten pounds."

In fact, Luke thinks everything I own costs about ten pounds, even my Kurt Geiger shoes. Equally, whenever he goes out with his mates it only ever costs him twenty quid even if he's been boozing all afternoon! I suppose our mutual white lies give us carte blanche to spend what we like.

Pat fondly remembered a hotel that he used to visit as a child when his parents came to the city to do their banking. It was called The Galle Face Hotel and he suggested that we go there to watch the sunset. The hotel was a pleasant retreat from the busy streets outside. Teenagers were enjoying a game of cricket on the long green lawn facing the sea, while others flew their kites in the gentle breeze. The contrast to the chaotic city was delightful.

Walking through the grand entrance, we arrived in a huge hall to be greeted by smartly dressed porters in white uniforms, with red embroidery on their lapels and epaulettes. With big welcoming smiles they guided us into the hotel's beautiful grounds facing the sea. Pat knew his way around and looked very much at home. He didn't say what emotions it provoked but I could tell he was reminiscing as he smiled to himself, soaking up the view. I didn't want to intrude on his thoughts.

We chose a table on the seafront and watched as the waves crashed against the rocks and the sea spray disappeared in the heat. The strong smell of seaweed filled my nostrils. It was spectacular. The sun was setting against a silhouette of palm trees. With a gin and tonic in hand I knew I was going to like it here.

"Are you happy Pat?" I asked.

"Very happy, my dear, it is exactly how I remember it," he replied, a beer in one hand and a cigar in the other.

As night fell we decided to walk back to the busy city to find somewhere to eat. The roads were utter chaos. There were buses, cars, lorries, tuk-tuks, bicycles, rickshaws and cows. Everywhere there were men on motorcycles with women sitting behind them, sideways on, their long saris trailing over the exhausts and their children perched precariously on the handle bars. There were five family members on one bike with boxes piled on their heads. The traffic was stationery with engines still running, black fumes pumping out of them. Everyone was thumping their horns. The noise was incredible and made my head spin. As soon as the traffic lights changed they were off, motorbikes revving their engines as they zipped in and out of the traffic and rubber tyres screeching. It was completely insane.

We walked along winding, dimly-lit streets, leisurely taking in our new environment. We were undecided about where to go until Pat shouted at us to wait. He had found another one of his childhood haunts and was beckoning to us excitedly.

"The Swimming Club!" he shouted.

Pat had learnt to swim here as a young boy, fifty years ago, but it was now a members-only club. At the reception we explained Pat's story and asked if we could have a quick peep. The man vanished to ask his boss and returned smiling.

"Come on in, you may look," he said.

We ambled into a grand hallway with dark, wood-panelled walls. The polished, colonial furniture reminded me of museums at home. You could tell the place was well looked after. Pat's excitement was evident as he recognised the names of old friends in lists of awards mounted in frames on the walls. In the moonlight, children ran around the swimming pools while well-to-do Sri Lankan families dined at candlelit tables.

Intrigued by eight pale foreigners, the boss of the club asked to talk with Pat. As they chatted, we loitered in the reception. To our surprise he invited us to have dinner. As we sat down by the swimming pools, among the Sri Lankan high society, we felt very privileged indeed. We enjoyed an evening of fine food and wine and it was moving to see Pat's eyes fill with happiness. I tried to imagine his life here, learning to swim while his parents cheered him on from the edge of the pool. This was Pat's first attempt to revisit his childhood and I couldn't imagine what emotions he must be feeling. This was once his life with his parents. Now he was here with his adult children, a parent himself and both of his parents gone.

We left the Swimming Club at midnight. The boss smiled and nodded his head, as we thanked him, patting Pat on the back in a friendly manner. Even if we never found anything else that Pat remembered, that night made our journey worthwhile; just to see his face.

The next morning after breakfast, we ventured into Colombo again. We spent hours shopping for fabrics and clothes. Luke and I managed to fit in a trip to the zoo, which we always try to do wherever we go. Colombo's zoo is set in tropical, botanical gardens full of evergreen jackfruit trees with the world's largest fruit, weighing up to 30kg. They had worked hard on the animals' enclosures and the beasts look well cared-for and content. The only area I found disturbing was the Big Cat enclosure, where all the different species were cramped next to one another in small cages. It looked like the Victorian photos of London Zoo's old cat house. I could only hope that this was on their list of site improvements. There are eighty-six native mammal species in Sri Lanka, from sloth bears and leopards to porcupines and dugongs, and I was hoping to see some of the wildlife when we left the city.

The school children visiting the zoo found Luke and I far more fascinating than the elephant show going on behind them. Slowly but surely a large crowd gathered around, pointing, laughing and talking about us. I tried to look through them at the elephant show. One of them pulled a face at me so I stuck out my tongue and crossed my eyes which made them scream.

As we left the zoo a middle-aged man ran towards us smiling and carrying a fir cone stuck on the end of a stick. He was really excited and kept shoving the cone under our noses, waving it around and sweeping the ground. I was baffled as to why he thought we would want to buy it. I felt guilty and looked at Luke who just said "No!" The man's smile turned to disappointment and his shoulders drooped as he walked away.

We got into a tuk-tuk that had careered towards us, still laughing about the fir cone, as we watched the man chase after some other poor soul who looked equally unimpressed by his gadget. As our tuk-tuks screeched off, we held onto our seats for another hair-raising experience.

4 – HEADING SOUTH

Christmas was creeping closer and it was time to head south to the beaches where we planned to chill-out and enjoy the festivities. After much discussion and seven different opinions we all agreed to go to Unawatuna, about five kilometres southeast of Galle. In the guidebook it is described as having a curving bay with a picturesque sweep of golden beach. I always enjoy the cultural side of travelling but after a hard year at work nothing fills me with more pleasure than the thought of a tropical beach.

Galle is Sri Lanka's fourth biggest town and is 116km from Colombo. At about the same size as Ireland, Sri Lanka's greatest length from north to south is 273 miles and its greatest width 137 miles. From Galle, the finest colonial city on the island, we would have to get another form of transport to the beaches on the southern tip but it would take only twenty minutes. One train and a short journey by taxi should be a breeze.

The next day, after a traditional Sri Lankan breakfast, we packed our bags, showered and headed for the train station. It was early, but hot already. The humid air was causing a film of sweat across my face. Wiping away the trickles that rolled past my ears had become second nature. We arrived at the train station, queued for our tickets and then made our way to the platform. Our train was called Samudradevi, 'Queen of the Sea', because of her daily journey up and down the coast of Sri Lanka. Everyone was helpful and friendly, asking where we were off to and offering advice on where to stay and what not to miss.

We walked onto the platform and it was immediately evident that this was going to be a crush. Hundreds of people already lined the platform; most of them seemed to own boxes upon boxes of luggage. What the hell was in them? It was like a huge, crazy market.

The beggars picked out our pale faces in the crowd and crawled towards us. They grabbed at our clothes, twisted hands with dirty fingernails reaching out to us. I gave them some change but the coins slipped through their fingers onto the floor. I felt pity as they scrabbled around for them. How can some people be destined for a life like this? It really is a lottery as to where you are born. The first time I saw badly crippled people was in India and it really disturbed me. I still think of one – a woman at Mumbai train station. She had no limbs, was tied to a skateboard by a rope, and had been pushed into the middle of the station where hundreds of people stepped over and threw money at her. She must have been scared, lying there alone, not able to eat, drink or go to the toilet. Who had put her there? We made eye contact and I remember looking at her tear-stained cheeks. I smiled at her and said hello. I remember the corners of her mouth moved as if she was grateful somebody had acknowledged her.

The old train was on the horizon. The locals were already moving towards the edge of the platform. There was no yellow line or any electronic voice reminding you to mind the gap. The noise was incredible; people shouting, horns beeping and the sound of the train's engine was deafening. As it pulled into the station I was amazed to see faces pressed up against the metal bars of the windows. They were hanging out of the doors, half-open, secured only by rope. My dream image of our coastal journey on the Queen of the Sea had been dashed.

Every time I turned around I had to keep apologising, "Sorry, sorry, sorry". My rucksack was banging into everybody, it felt like it was full of bricks and was stuck to my hot sweaty back. I know when I pack my bags before holidays that I won't wear half of the stuff that I take but I always get carried away. I had even brought a size ten pair of shorts! I don't think I've been a size ten since I was sixteen. My wardrobe includes clothes of all shapes and sizes because I always hope that I will fit into them again one day.

How the hell were we going to get on this bloody train? "Ouch. Ow. Bollocks!" Somebody had trodden on my toes. I yelped and gritted my teeth. Why the hell do toes hurt so much? "Shit. Bollocks. Ouch!" I limped along not daring to check whether my toenails had been pulled off. Luke shot me a look and told me to stop swearing. I didn't try to explain and pulled a face at him.

It was hard to keep my cool, as bony elbows dug into my ribs and I was pushed and shoved around. Everyone had one goal – to board this train. I was starting to lose the plot. Feeling anger starting to rise, I grimaced. People's faces came at me, exhaling hot breath. Smiling like Cheshire cats, they asked the same question over and over again:

"What's your name, where you come from?"

I replied through gritted teeth, "Tracey, England," not wanting to offend these smiling strangers.

There was no time for pleasantries, we were on a mission. The humidity and the smell of diesel were making me choke. There was only one way of getting on this train and that was to join the surge. No more apologies, it was time to put our heads down and push our way along with the others.

Eventually we were on! All seven of us clambered up the ladders and fell inside. I had imagined the train to be similar to the Indian trains I had travelled on; comfy and spacious, with a window seat, and the opportunity to soak up the Sri Lankan countryside while sampling different foods. Instead there was only one space left. This was for a very good reason; it was by the toilet and standing room only.

It was crowded, noisy and dirty. The final straw was when I was shoved for the hundredth time and a bottle of suntan lotion burst all over my trousers. I was covered. We all laughed loudly. I suppose it made the train smell better, temporarily. I managed to check my throbbing toes and was relieved that there was no blood, but they were painful and looked bruised already.

The train started and so did the continuous flow of toilet users. Every time the door opened, a putrid smell gusted out. We all shrieked covering our faces with tissues and gagged as a mixture of sick, urine and faeces penetrated our nostrils. This was not the journey we had envisaged, but there was nothing we could do.

The Sri Lankan commuters were amused at our retching by the loo. The women shyly watched us and giggled. I imagined myself stooping over the hole in the floor, losing my balance, and sliding through all the mess on the floor. I would have to wet myself rather than go in there.

Crushed against the side of a wall with a dripping roof was no fun. We were rocking from side to side with the motion of the train, swaying against strangers as if dancing in a crowd at Glastonbury. My clothes were stuck to me and my hair was wet. Every time somebody needed to get past, I got another jab in the ribs and I tried to keep my toes tightly curled up and out of the way.

Smiling men carrying baskets of food on their heads pushed their way along the corridors shouting out their culinary delights as they went by. I'm sure it was delicious but eating next to a toilet wasn't on the agenda for me. Luke is over six feet tall and was repeatedly bashed in the head by the baskets. Every time he took a deep breath and raised his eyebrows with a wry smile.

Eventually we managed to press our way along the mobbed corridor towards a gap by the door. Fresh air at last! I would rather take my chances with the open door than stand by the toilet. I never imagined I would be so grateful to lean out of a train door speeding along. I would never do this on the London to Birmingham train but here I was more than happy to risk it.

Every time I made eye contact with somebody, they would say the same thing:

"What's your name, where you come from?"

I wanted to say, "Piss off and leave me alone, can't you see I am sweaty, tired, the train stinks and I don't want a stupid pointless conversation with you!" Instead I simply smiled again and said, "Tracey, England," but I never received a reply. They just continued staring. We would stand there like two idiots smiling at one another uncomfortably until the next passenger made eye contact and the same question and answer were exchanged.

A trendy young Sri Lankan man joined us. He had slicked back hair and wore a shiny cream suit and lots of aftershave. His English was amazing but I was immediately suspicious of his insincere eyebrows, moving rapidly up and down, and the cheesy grin he pulled as he dragged on a fag and blew the smoke straight into our faces. He was too familiar. I guessed where the conversation would end up as soon as he hunted us out. He owned a gem shop. The poor bloke spent a good hour chatting, grooming us, and telling us that he was our friend for life and that he was coming to stay with us in England, before he slipped this into the conversation. He wanted us to buy gems off him. These carried as much appeal as a fir cone on a stick.

He was persuasive, though, and got me dancing with him while he sang a Ricky Martin number; "Upside, inside out, she's livin' la vida loca, she'll push and pull you down, livin la vida loca, her lips are devil red and her skin's the colour mocha, la, la, la." He stretched out his right leg, twisting his foot and gyrating his hips, running his hands through his greasy hair, pouting. It must have been heat stroke, but I grooved on down with him, shocked that he knew all these words to this song – I didn't. Eventually, when he realised that we weren't going to buy anything from him, he left us and moved along the train towards two young western girls. I saw the one facing us look deflated and her eyes glazed over as he started his spiel. She didn't jump up to dance with him.

Apart from the madness, the view out of the door was amazing and as the warm air blew into my face, I began to relax. Leaving the outskirts of Colombo, the sides of the railway tracks were crowded with shanty towns. Some of the shelters were made only of cardboard and rope. Elderly people sat outside on the hard, dry ground looking glum. I felt awkward as they watched us tourists on our way to the coast, reminding them of their poverty.

The children stood and watched in amazement as the old train chugged past them. They laughed and waved enthusiastically, running alongside the long train until they couldn't keep up and dropped behind. We waved back at them. Some toddlers, wearing only nappies, stood alone. At least they weren't working on the trains like some of the kids in India, I thought. Three year olds crawling around on the floor, polishing it with rags, under your feet, tapping your legs asking for money and miming that they needed food.

Adults squatted, their long robes ruffled over their arms, exposing their bums and emptying their bowels at the side of the track. The first time I saw this in India I was disgusted. I mean if somebody defecated in St Pancras station, next to the champagne bar, you wouldn't just accept it and look away would you? But I soon became immune to it.

Once out of the city, it was a breath taking view. The turquoise sea sparkled in the sun and there were miles of golden sand fringed with palm trees. I could see fishermen in their brightly painted boats dragging their nets onto the deck. We passed clumps of huts with smoke billowing out of from their roofs. Colourful washing hung outside, blowing in the sea air, while naked children played cricket on the beach. I could smell burning wood and cooking. We passed people in big sun hats working in hundreds of neatly designed paddy fields – they were the most luscious shades of green. The heat shimmered from the ground and the hills behind made the whole scene look like a film set.

Farmers whipped water buffalo, dragging massive ploughs behind them and I thought how hard their lives were compared to the two water buffalo I had worked with at Howletts' Zoo when I was young. Their names were Hagimar and Blackie and they would throw spectacular tantrums if you were late with their breakfast. There is no way they would have coped with this harsh lifestyle. I smiled to myself as I remembered them fondly with their big wet noses and fluffy cheeks.

Hundreds of elegant white cattle egret followed the farmers while they worked on the land, and Brahimy kites soared high in the sky above the fields. The sun caught their wings and made them glisten. Little green Bee eaters sat on the telephone wires waiting to hunt the insects that filled the sky. Already, there was an abundance of wildlife and I couldn't wait to explore.

We pulled into various train stations along the way. Each station name was written in the fancy swirls of the Sinhalese alphabet. I reckoned it would be a hard language to learn to write. People on the platforms tried to sell us things – windup toys, lighters, and little fans – or just asked us our names. The heat was incredible when the train was stationery and I was glad of the breeze each time it pulled away. I was enjoying being by the open door. Work and London were fast becoming a distant memory.

5 – UNAWATUNA – ZIMMER REST AND THE VILLAGE INN

Arriving in Galle we needed a minibus to take us on to Unawatuna and our final destination, 'Zimmer Rest', which Fran had picked. Leaving the train proved to be as difficult as getting on. People were climbing over us in their haste. Once off, the usual procedure began as touts grabbed at our bags desperate to get us into a vehicle and to their guest house. We had to explain over and over that we had a place. They continued to argue amongst themselves and pushed one another around. In all the commotion they weren't even listening to us. My rucksack was repeatedly yanked which quickly became unbearable. Pat strode out of the station into the street where he found a bus for us and we all piled in, hot, sweaty and slightly irritated. A tout climbed in and insisted on staying with us for the journey. Every now and then he turned around and flashed us a smile, exposing his rotten teeth. His breath was as bad as the toilet on the train.

We arrived at Zimmer Rest and were greeted by Thalik, its friendly owner. He had a kind, calm presence. He was in his early fifties with short cropped hair and a wiry physique. He wore a Western-style cotton shirt, shorts and flip flops. Unbeknown to us then, this man was to become our friend and help us through some very difficult times ahead. Pat paid our bus driver and he left with the tout still sitting beside him.

Zimmer Rest was set in pretty tropical gardens with neatly trimmed borders and its dusty paths were swept so as to leave patterns in the dirt. The furniture was made of very dark teak, the same style as the Swimming Club in Colombo, and the walls were a shrine to hundreds of Sri Lankan masks, which were for sale. Huge palms and banana plants framed the veranda; there were chess and backgammon tables and a library of Buddhist books and maps to browse through. Thalik was thrilled that we were admiring his hard work. His pride and joy was a huge painting of Sri Lankan women picking tea leaves in the hills; it reminded me of our PG Tips boxes at home. Every day Thalik asked if I wanted to buy it.

Although the building was beautiful and inviting, I had set my heart on a beach hut. I had been looking forward to going to sleep listening to the gentle sound of the waves lapping the sand. Luke and I decided to go in search of one. Duncan, Camille and Saskia came with us.

We cut through a side street that led onto the beach. It really was paradise. It was exactly as the book had described – a sweeping bay of white sand with a crystal blue sea. There was a temple on the rocks overlooking the bay. The palm trees looked as if they had been artistically planted to frame the shore. The beach bars were settled neatly on the sand with a variety of culinary delights to sample. Multi-coloured fabrics danced in the breeze alongside handmade trousers and skirts, and smiling women beckoned us to look at their wares. People were splashing around in the sea and playing volleyball on the soft white sand.

Other traders were carrying heavy baskets laden with goods to buy. They were selling the strangest of things. One old man tried to get us to buy maracas. He was shaking them at us as he leant on his walking stick. He had hardly any teeth and those he did have were stained bright orange and looked like miniature tombstones. I watched him limp away with his heavy basket, using his stick to keep his balance. I vowed I would buy a pair of his maracas before we left.

The beach traders stopped at every single table and sun lounger along the beach, in the hope of selling something. They would be greeted by people shaking their heads and saying that they didn't want any but it didn't seem to bother them and they would walk off smiling.

Everyone seemed happy. Tourists sunbathed and read books, their white complexions matching the sand, or sat at tables under the palms with beers and various cocktails, playing cards, or backgammon. The vibe was good. A group of scuba divers were loading their equipment onto a boat.

We looked out at the sea – the tops of snorkels poked out of the crystal water with flippered feet splashing behind them. The surface of the water shimmered and we had to squint and put our hands to our brows to shade us from the glare of the sun. The fishermen tended to their nets laid out on the sand. Low music could be heard floating from a few of the bars and the ambience was dreamy.

This was definitely heaven. A wave of happiness washed over me. I had read in our Lonely Planet guide that Marco Polo, the globetrotting explorer, thought Sri Lanka was the finest island of its size in the entire world. From what I had already seen I agreed with him. It is also described as the teardrop of India falling from its southern end. It hangs like a pendant, alone in the ocean.

We kicked off our flip flops and sunk our feet into the soft sand. My bruised toes and ankles swollen from the flight were a sight to behold but I didn't care – the warm sand was comforting and I massaged my tired feet. The waves gently lapped on the beach and I watched them, mesmerised. I recalled that the bay is famous for safe swimming – the reef protects the bay so the currents are slow.

We searched for a couple of hours for a beach hut. I was limping, my toes were swelling. We hadn't considered that the huts would be fully booked with city people coming down to celebrate Christmas. Traipsing in and out of various apartments and beach huts in the blazing sun was hard work. We heard the same answer over and over from the owners of each place – after Boxing Day rooms would be available. After trawling along the beach, in and out of bars and bungalows, we gave up and decided to do as they suggested and find a hut the day after Boxing Day.

Disappointed, we returned to the beach and found a table under the palms to wait for Pat and Fran. We ordered ice cold beers and soaked up our new surroundings. After a dip in the ocean we felt refreshed so Luke and I decided to try one last time to find a place to stay. We set off in a different direction and stumbled across the 'Village Inn' set back from the beach.

We walked down a narrow path lined with tropical fauna and flora, into a pretty garden draped in cerise and magenta bougainvillea and beautiful ginger plants. It was quiet, apart from the flocks of Blossom-headed parakeets squawking away in the jungle trees. The owner came out to greet us with a broad smile and introduced himself. Dammika was barefoot and wearing only a dhoti, a traditional cloth wrapped around his middle and tied in a knot, which showed off his muscular, toned body. His wife stood behind him, also smiling, and holding their young son who had a chubby, happy face and a cute bowl haircut.

We asked him if he had any rooms. We had spotted a lovely hut, set amidst the tropical vegetation, as we walked into the grounds. It had a veranda with table and chairs and, although not facing the sea, it was enchanting. I immediately asked whether the hut was available but Dammika told us that it was saved for his relatives who were coming to stay for Christmas. Another hut, with an old man in a white vest sitting outside on the veranda, was his dad's house. I tried not to look too disappointed as he took us to view his other rooms. I could feel 'spoilt brat' rearing her ugly head and was desperately trying to suppress her.

Dammika led us to the first floor of a small house, his bare feet slapping on the concrete. Red ants were forming orderly lines on the stairwell. I tried not to step on them. It was fascinating to watch them carrying things like a tiny army. The room had a balcony overlooking the jungle with tables and chairs. It had the prerequisite mosquito net, a fan and an en-suite bathroom. It was immaculate and smelt nice and clean. Although very different from what we had expected we decided to take it. Dammika was very happy and called down to his wife who started collecting clean sheets for us.

I think fate had led us to this place. This sturdy, concrete building would later save our lives and those of others.

We went back to Zimmer Rest to collect our rucksacks and explain to Thalik what we were doing. We apologized, but he didn't seem bothered. We trudged back carrying our heavy rucksacks along the winding paths to Village Inn with the sun beating down on us. The rest of the family had decided to stay at Zimmer Rest and we were only a twenty minute walk away so everyone was happy. I love Luke's family like my own but I thought it would be good to have some space away.

I sat on the balcony while Luke had a shower and kicked off my flip flops. The concrete floor was painted a rusty colour, was cool to touch, and felt very soothing. I filled a bowl with cold water and shower gel to try and get the swelling down on my ankles and toes. I plopped my feet into the bowl and admired the view into the jungle. Leaning back in my chair I browsed through the book of visitors' comments. The air was full of the calls of the birds in the jungle.

As I flicked through the pages of the visitors' book I noticed everybody had the same comments about Village Inn. I read that they had loved staying here, that the family was very kind and hospitable, and that it was a peaceful retreat from the beach nestled in the jungle. Some guests actually visited on a regular basis. It might not be a beach hut but I knew we would enjoy staying here. I watched a flock of multi-coloured butterflies flutter by, landing on some big orange trumpet flowers to suck the nectar. They looked magical.

We spent the next few days relaxing on the beach unwinding after our busy year. Nathan had arrived from Thailand and looked healthy and bronzed from his travels. It was great to see him again and we had lots of catching up to do. We chatted for hours, taking the piss out of one another, laughing and having fun. We played Travel Scrabble and our favourite game, Articulate. I bought some beautiful fabrics and various items from the beach traders, much to Luke's annoyance, and of course we enjoyed refreshing ourselves with cold beer in the late afternoon. We all teased Saskia who has a phobia of snakes. She was terrified of the Sri Lankan men on the beach who carried huge pythons and cobras around all day, wanting you to have a photo taken with the poor animals.

As a child, on hot summer afternoons, I spent endless hours lying on the grass in my Nan's back garden with my sister Dawn making images out of clouds, so when Nathan pointed out the shape of a huge white dove over the bay it reminded me of my childhood innocence. It was the only cloud in the sky and the dove's wings seemed to be protecting the bay.

"A good sign for an amazing holiday," said Nathan, and we all agreed.

Our evenings were spent trying new curries, washed down with plenty of wine, while exchanging stories about the past year. This holiday was turning out to be just perfect. Each night, Luke and I returned to the Village Inn and before we went to bed we always made sure to say goodnight to the old man sitting on the veranda in his white vest.

6 – SUNIL'S RESTAURANT

The evening before Christmas Eve we stumbled upon a makeshift restaurant. It was set on a small road off the beach, lit up with fairy lights and surrounded by the biggest rubber plants I had ever seen. We walked in and were greeted by a long-haired guy, wearing shorts and a scruffy t-shirt. He came over to us clutching some menus and told us we could sit wherever we liked.

We chose a table, ordered some drinks and settled in there for the evening. The menu offered an array of traditional, mouth-watering Sri Lankan dishes. Excitedly we read through the list, drooling over the descriptions of every offering. The smell of fried garlic and chilli from the kitchen only increased our hunger and so we ordered a wide selection. The devilled chicken and prawns were hot and spicy, infused with chilli – this is one of Sri Lanka's fieriest dishes – it sets your taste buds on fire. Rice is a staple food and locally caught fish were served in a superb coconut based curry sauce with chilli and tiny curry leaves that brought beads of sweat to our foreheads.

As four of us are vegetarian so we ordered plenty of vegetable dishes to share; mainly curries in different sauces. Sri Lankan curries are made with coconut milk, sliced onion, green chilli, spices such as cloves and nutmeg, cinnamon, saffron and aromatic leaves. On offer were delights such as cashew nut curry, eggplant curry, curried okra, bean curry, and spicy potatoes to name a few. These were served with seeni sambal, a hot sweet coconut paste. Sugar is added to take the sting out of the chilli.

The parripu – a hot red lentil dhal served with rice – and the vegetarian Indian thali- a selection of little tin pots, each one containing a different curry – were personal favourites. Potatoes and pumpkins were fried and served with thin gravies known as hodi. Sweet coconut chutneys came with dosa breads to dip into the tins, and this is a much easier way to eat a thali than with rice.

Dining etiquette in Sri Lanka is the same as in India. You eat using your fingers. The main difference is that in India you have lots of curry with a small helping of rice. In Sri Lanka you have vast portions of rice (or bread) with smaller portions of curry. You mould the rice into little mouth-sized parcels and then dip it into the sauces. Sri Lankans have it down to a fine art but eating like this sitting around the table with Luke and his brothers was a sight to behold; their faces covered in curry and more food on the table than in their stomachs. At least they tried. I chose to eat with a spoon, but maybe I missed out.

After a lovely feast and a few bottles of locally made Lion lager, we were all stuffed. Luke's parents, Camille and Saskia went to bed. Luke, Duncan, Nathan and I decided to stay and sample the local arrack made from coconuts. You drink it with cola and it tastes similar to Tia Maria, very sweet and smooth. Sunil, the owner, invited us to join him and his friends for a late-night drinking session. He was very generous and I warmed to him straight away. Sunil had a good business head on him and his bar was stylish, built around trees, and with subtle lighting. Laidback, with long, unruly hair, Sunil evidently liked his drink and smoked heavily. He made huge fat spliffs, leant back in his chair and puffed away like a steam train. His eyes narrowed and he smiled as he blew smoke rings. Bob Marley played in the background. Funny wherever you travel Bob can always be heard singing in the background.

An old man, dressed in the traditional Sri Lankan dhoti, joined our table. He started to make the most incredible tunes by tapping his fingers and wrists on the table. I listened in amazement. He must have been doing this since he was a child. The force with which he hit the wood with the tips of his fingers made me flinch, as it looked painful, but it didn't seem to bother him in the slightest. I tapped my feet in time to the rhythm. We all ended up singing and dancing. I think the arrack helped!

He got each of us to create different beats on the table with our fingers and the palms of our hands. It was fun as we made mistakes and laughed. It was like playing the bongos. Duncan rapped with them and they nicknamed him Rap Attack. They kept shouting for more drinks as they danced – a mixture of traditional Sri Lankan and western movements. The Arrack and Coke kept flowing and the trays laden with glasses kept arriving.

Sunil talked about having lived by the sea all his life. He said that in thirty-three years he had never known the water to be as choppy as it was that day and that other local people and fishermen had also commented on it.

He proudly showed us photos of his infant son and talked about his wife Helga. He promised we would meet his little boy tomorrow. He was keen to show him off to us. We were all quite tiddly at this point, so it was one more Arrack for the road and then we all sloped off to bed in the early hours. Weaving our way along the road in the humid night heat, laughing and chattering, I kissed Nathan and Duncan goodnight and they headed off to Zimmer Rest while we walked back to Village Inn.

The old man in his vest, sitting on the veranda, nodded goodnight to us as we climbed the stairs to our bedroom.

7 – CHRISTMAS EVE AND CHRISTMAS DAY

Christmas Eve was spent on the beach. We enjoyed a very lazy day, reading, swimming, drinking beer and snoozing before taking up residence under the shade of the palms. We decided to go back to Sunil's for dinner that evening as we had enjoyed ourselves so much the night before.

As the sun dropped to the horizon Luke and I went to his favourite roti bar which was a dilapidated little shack on the beach and ordered two cold Lion lagers and a vegetable and meat roti. Rotis or short eats are small doughy parcels with a kick, filled with anything that takes your fancy – meat, fish, or vegetables. Luke loves them. We sat on the plastic chairs in the sand, put our beers on the wonky table and watched the dogs running up and down the beach, playing together. I watched as the sun dropped towards the straight line of the ocean, until only an orange-skin shaped smile was left and it faded away to light another country's day.

We went to shower and tidy ourselves up before dinner. My face looked quite burnt in the mirror as I put on my mascara, so I vowed to wear more suntan lotion tomorrow. Luke and I strolled along to meet the rest of the family. It was a beautiful evening. The warmth of the dusty ground was soothing on our feet as we walked in the twilight. The sky was full of stars flickering against the navy blue sky. I held Luke's hand and felt incredibly happy to be there.

Sunil was pleased to see us and prepared a table; we were treated like royalty. The chef came out to greet us, laughing about the night before and frantically shaking our hands. I felt slightly embarrassed that we had made such fools of ourselves, dancing around the restaurant, but they didn't seem to care. We ordered a bottle of wine. That's the funny thing about booze. You deny that you have a hangover then the horrors of the night before come back to haunt you. You try not to remember what an idiot you were, and pretend, 'Who, me?' I sipped my wine and slowly felt better.

Luke's family arrived, looking healthy and relaxed. We ordered various dishes and comfortably settled ourselves in for the evening. Sitting under the moon for our meal surrounded by fairy lights was simply perfect. The air was filled with the sounds of crickets and geckos chirping.

Sunil walked across his restaurant and proudly introduced us to his beautiful son as he had promised. He was cute and unusual looking; a mix of white European and Sri Lankan. We all watched him as he played by a Christmas tree with an inflatable Santa. He captured the attention of all around him. His mother Helga proudly told us how he had chosen the lights himself from the local shop. She lifted him up so that he could point out which ones he had picked. He poked the multi-coloured bulbs and chuckled to himself. His mother whispered something into his ear and snuggled into him. Laughing, she put him down and he skipped off, twirling around and giggling. She was so proud and his smile was enchanting. He looked like a little angel dressed in his white Christmas outfit. He danced around the tables, smiling and waving.

After dinner we decided to go down to the beach for a few drinks and on to a party. We sat at the bar we frequented day and night whether for breakfast or evening meal, we liked it here. The waiters at the Hot Rock were all young lads, friendly and attentive. In the morning, they always put towels on the sun loungers to save them for us. I bet onlookers thought we were German. We never asked them to do this but I suppose a family of eight eating and drinking all day was quite an income for them so it was in their best interest. The waiters greeted us excitedly and brought candles and buckets of ice straight over. They flashed their cheeky smiles, especially at young, blonde Saskia. We giggled when Camille pointed out that one of the older lads, a handsome skinhead, had taken a shine to her. He was gorgeous. Saskia smiled at him and he became all bashful.

The moon sparkled on the sea and a sea breeze blew gently through my hair cooling me down. I felt relaxed and content with life. Every night the whole beach was candlelit and as it was Christmas Eve another surprise was in store for us. Children began to light fireworks, shrieking with delight as they soared from their hands. Pat joined in and aimed some across the sea with the children. He probably used to do this as a child. We sat drinking wine and listening to the waves breaking on the sand, gazing at the palms silhouetted against the moon.

As it was Christmas Eve we decided to explore the beach parties. We waved goodnight to our waiters and said:

"See you in the morning."

They waved back. We found ourselves at the Happy Banana, a popular beach bar, where we all drank far too much. Fran and Camille danced the night away with the local boys while Pat snored over his glass of beer, which wasn't unusual – he can sleep anywhere – it's his party trick. Eventually we all decided that Pat had the right idea. It was time for bed so we left at some point in the early morning. We staggered off towards the

Village Inn, shouting our goodbyes to the rest of the family as they weaved along the road towards Zimmer Rest.

As we walked down the familiar path, the little flicker of the old man's candle welcomed us.

"Goodnight," we called, and he nodded back.

I awoke on Christmas Day with blurred vision underneath my mosquito net. The fan whooshed above me and watching its arms go round and round made me feel even worse. It was already hot and the fan merely circulated the warm air around the room. I untangled myself from the net and went to the bathroom.

As I brushed my teeth and glugged the warm, bottled water, swilling it around my mouth, I began to feel better. I turned on the shower and stood with my face under it, trying to wash away the cobwebs. When I opened the balcony door I felt uplifted by the view of the jungle as the new day began. The sun's rays were breaking through the palms and although there was no breeze it was cooler outside than in our room. I watched Dammika's wife hang out her washing and a prehistoric-looking monitor lizard take his morning dip in the stream. The birds were chirping and the distant calls of the toque macaques filled the jungle.

A group of Italian travellers arrived asking for rooms but Dammika sent them away as he was full. I was relieved that we had a place and, looking down from my lovely balcony, felt sorry for them. Christmas really was a very busy time down on the coast. Just like Mary and Joseph looking for a room at the inn, everywhere was full. There was a rumour going round that some tourists had no choice but to sleep on the beach until after Boxing Day.

"Happy Christmas!" shouted Luke.

"Happy Christmas to you too." I said.

Luke got up and after he'd showered we sat down in the garden for our breakfast amid the tropical plants. Fresh tea with sugar warmed our dry throats. Dammika brought us fried eggs and crusty toast. We had to go to Zimmer Rest to meet the family for our Christmas celebrations. The walk felt much longer than usual as we trudged under the hot sun, not really talking, clutching our neatly wrapped Christmas presents. Everyone we met along the way looked the same, wearing big shades, glum expressions, and carrying a fizzy drink. The sun's rays were strong even through my sunglasses.

I knew that the day was going to be spent nursing hangovers and opening the presents we had all brought with us from England, Japan and Thailand. As we walked through the big wrought iron gates, we could see the family on Thalik's veranda. They were still having their breakfast. Everyone looked slightly jaded.

"Happy Christmas," we called.

We put our presents on the table and Thalik, bare-chested and wearing only shorts, watched with wonder at this strange tradition and the unwrapping of gifts we had brought. I think he found it all rather peculiar, but asked us for the wrapping paper which we happily gave him.

The strangest present was the one I had for Luke. My plan had been to buy his presents at the duty free shops in England but of course with all the hassle at the airport there had been no time to look around. I had then shot straight to the shops in Dubai airport while we waited for our connecting flight to Sri Lanka. If you liked badly carved camels with saddles covered in gold stitching or tacky clothes with camel prints on them, this was your place. Don't get me wrong, I love camels and work with three very special Bactrian ladies at the zoo – Nina, Nadia and Noeime – but I think even they would have turned up their noses at the appalling choice of gifts. I had started to panic and headed to the book department. We had two kittens at home and I remembered Luke saying he wanted to get a book on cats to understand these two little mites better. Jumping out from the shelf was a cat book! After paying for it at the till, I shoved the book into a carrier bag, feeling pleased with myself. I ran to find the rest of the gang and whispered to Camille that I had Luke's present. She looked at it and laughed. It was called *Cat Confidential* and was written by an eccentric woman who gave all sorts of nonsensical advice. Poor Luke opened his present to the sniggers of all around him. Luckily, he saw the funny side. This book was to help us through difficult moments as we read chapters out to one another and laughed. The madness of *Cat Confidential* would end up keeping us sane.

Christmas Day was a bit of a flop because of our excessive alcohol consumption the night before. Luke's family decided to go on a glass-bottomed boat trip for some snorkelling. I decided against this, given my pounding head, and thought them brave to be embarking on this sort of adventure with hangovers. I waved them off and settled down in the shade with my book and a fresh banana milkshake. They returned later, green-faced and staggering along the beach. I was in hysterics as Duncan weaved towards me, with his sea legs and missed his chair and went to the bar toilets to be sick. After chilling on the beach for the afternoon we headed back to our rooms for showers before our Christmas dinner.

I called my mum from a local internet café to wish the family a happy Christmas and told her that we were on a beautiful beach on the south coast. The line was very bad and, with the added delay after speaking it was a rather disjointed conversation. I rambled on about how idyllic it was, what a great time we were having, blah blah. We wished one another a happy Christmas and hung up. Little did I know that the memory of this phone call was to cause great distress to family and friends back home over the next few days.

Christmas dinner was eaten and more cava was consumed.

"See you on the beach in the morning," we called to Luke's family as we left.

As we headed back we saw a London couple, Christine and her husband. They looked really drunk.

He raised his big glass of Bailey's and slurred, "Aren't we lucky?"

I smiled and said, "Yes we are. Happy Christmas," knowing that he would be feeling like me in the morning.

Luke fell straight to sleep and I began to read a book that my sister Dawn had given me, *P.S I love you*, about a young woman whose husband dies and leaves her notes to help her through the next twelve months. It made me feel quite sad. I looked at Luke sleeping and kissed his shoulder goodnight. I put the book down and turned the light off.

8 – BOXING DAY: THE TSUNAMI

I suddenly felt very nervous, as though there was a lot of commotion going on around me. As I opened my eyes I thought I could see shadows of people and my anxiety increased. I quickly closed my eyes and opened them again. What the hell was going on? I squinted to try and see more clearly – I could make out shapes at the end of my bed. I knew this made no logical sense. It looked like the outline of five, maybe six, figures and they were chattering. I couldn't work out what they were saying; it was too confusing. They seemed to be moving around in a clump and waving their arms about.

Fear gripped me as I realised something weird was going on. I hoped I was imagining it because I was tired and hung-over. I drew the sheet over my head like a child and quickly pulled my feet away from the end of the bed just in case something grabbed them. I was frightened and my heart was thumping in my chest. I reached out from under my protective sheet and put on the lamp. The light was comforting and I slowly pulled the sheet away from my face and sat there for a while to see if 'they' would appear again.

I felt safer with the light on and so decided to read while trying to make sense of what had just happened. Nobody will believe me, they will think I'm mad, I thought. I carried on reading until I fell asleep at around 3.30am which is why I overslept the next morning and was not on the beach.

Whatever I saw in my room that night saved my life. I am absolutely convinced that they came to warn me of the dangers ahead. I have always liked to imagine that there are guardian angels watching over us; now I really believe they do.

***

I woke in confusion and panic to the sound of a terrifying roar. I thought a plane was crashing. It was the same deafening sound a plane's engines make just before take-off. As I jumped up from under the mosquito net, I looked at the clock. It was 9.20am.

"Luke, Luke, wake up!" I screamed.

I ran to our balcony door and peered outside. On my left I could see a Sri Lankan woman looking up at the sky with horror in her eyes. I will never forget her – the fear in her face let me know something bad was happening. She started to run, screaming and tripping over her sari. She was being washed along by shallow water. She fell, twisting and turning, grabbing at plants, unable to get to her feet. I remember thinking that maybe a stream had burst, before losing sight of her in the jungle. I felt the house tremble.

The noise of a plane, rushing water; it didn't make sense.

Luke was still fast asleep. Later, he said he could hear a tremendous roaring but didn't want to wake up because he was so tired.

I shouted to Luke, "Flood! Get up, get up now! Fucking get up now, please, help!" Finally he opened his eyes and looked at me. I was frantically running in and out of the room.

"There's a flood, a mudslide, I don't know," I screamed. "Oh my God! Oh my God!"

I knew it was bad; every primitive instinct in my body told me so. I didn't know what it was but the survival instinct had kicked in, although all I was doing was running backwards and forwards.

"Mexico had mudslides, I saw it, I saw it on telly!" I was shouting, imagining us being engulfed and everything collapsing around us.

Luke jumped out of bed. He had never heard me shouting like this before and, disorientated, ran to see for himself.

The water was ankle-deep and streaming through the jungle. Luke tried to understand what he was seeing. Then the water sprayed around our house as if it was just a rock in the path of a wave. I screamed and jumped backwards. Terror hit me, I was panicking and gibbering. Luke realising it was bad, ran onto the balcony. The water was rising rapidly. It was rushing into the small stream in Dammika's garden and spreading out as far as the eye could see. Luke's first thought was the same as mine. It was a flood.

The roaring noise was overwhelming – it felt like the end of the world had come. The water looked dirty as it swirled past us with great force. It was rising fast. I was terrified. I didn't want to die like this.

I screamed at Luke, "What the hell is it, please tell me, please?" I was trembling and sobbing.

He shouted, "I don't know," as he ran back inside to pull on his shorts.

Once inside, Luke caught sight of the water, from another angle, through the window. He realised by its depth, the nature of the disaster unfolding before his eyes. It suddenly dawned on him that this could be a tsunami. He was trying to keep me calm as I had gone into shock but he knew that he had to tell me.

"It's a tsunami, it's a fucking tidal wave!" he shouted over the roar.

By the time he had pulled on his shorts the water was right up to our balcony; at least twelve to thirteen feet high.

"I don't understand. What are we going to do? Oh my God, Oh my God!" I cried.

"Hang on, calm down, shut up, stop screaming for fuck's sake," Luke shouted.

We heard more crashing and looked towards the sea. Another surge of water was heading our way through the palm trees. I started screaming again. The water around us pushed further into the jungle, carrying debris with it. I was hysterical now. Like a massive swollen river bursting its banks, the water took everything in its path. Plastic sun beds, tables, umbrellas, cars, cookers, pots and pans, fridges, planks of wood.

"Please do something, do something!" I begged Luke. My legs had turned to jelly and I thought I am going to die.

Luke saw a house collapse.

He looked up at the huge roof above us and decided we would be safer in the water but he also knew it would be hard persuading me to get in there. He could see that our house might collapse next, but his main mission was to keep me calm by repeating that it would be all right and we weren't going to die (although he really wasn't sure). From that moment, time stopped still and everything blurred. I had thought a tidal wave was several huge waves, but this was a massive wall of water. It was one of my biggest fears and I felt shattered.

I watched in terror as water swept across the land, taking everything with it – now I could see cars, vans, tuk-tuks, and water buffalo – and the tremendous roaring was the most frightening sound I'd ever heard. I couldn't comprehend what was unfolding before me. I stood silently, thinking blankly, we need an escape route.

I kept whispering over and over again, "A tsunami, a tsunami," trying to understand what this meant.

I don't think I had ever heard this word before. Searching for an explanation, I remained frozen. I couldn't think straight, gripped by fear, my brain was unable to digest what my eyes were seeing.

This is it, I'm going to die, right here, right now, in this black wave.

Now we were both panicking. Luke realised we were in trouble.

I began to pray. I'm not religious but thought it might help. I dropped to my knees. My legs had given way. I prayed over and over again, "don't let us die, please don't let us die," like a mantra, cupping my face with my trembling hands.

At first the pounding in our eardrums overwhelmed any noise from survivors. It seemed like we stood there for an eternity, watching the water rush past. It was like a biblical scene unfolding around us, and we waited to be swept away.

Even though Luke was there, I felt alone, as if I was preparing myself for death. You enter the world alone and maybe this is how your brain reacts when you are about to leave.

I shouted to Luke, "What are we going to do, oh my God."

BANG. Another house was washed away. I jumped out of my skin, my whole body was shaking. Luke didn't answer me. He just stood there in silence, watching. I was filled with panic and disbelief.

The water kept rushing by for what seemed like an eternity and then it started to slow down. As suddenly as it had arrived it stopped, as if somebody had pushed hard on the brake pedal. This was followed by an eerie silence. All I could hear was my heart thumping and, amazingly, birds singing in the trees.

Debris lay everywhere, cars and vans had been thrown around like Matchbox toys. There were terrifying sounds of houses creaking, crashing and then collapsing into the water like dominoes. Fridges and cookers bobbed on top of the water. We knew people would be trapped inside the houses but there was nothing we could do. The water was the same height as the eaves on the bungalow facing us. Miraculously it was still standing.

We stood there, not speaking. What would happen next?

Then blood-curdling screams brought us back to reality. I looked down from the balcony and saw people floundering in the water. Luke immediately leant over and stretched out his arms to help the victims as I stood there unable to move and barely registering what he was doing.

He shouted at me to help him.

I walked towards him, my legs trembling. Luke was yelling at me to get a grip but I was still in shock. I pulled myself together, leant over the balcony and grabbed somebody's arm. Luke held the other arm.

We pulled up two teenagers, brother and sister. They were both trembling and were badly grazed. Through chattering teeth the lad told us they had lost their mum, dad and baby brother, Harry. The terror in their eyes is something I will never forget and hopefully never see again as long as I live. They pleaded with me to try and find their parent and brother but there was nothing we could do. We didn't know what would happen next. I could barely stand up on my own two feet.

Then their mum appeared in the water. The kids started screaming at her:

"Mum, mum, over here!"

She looked up and swam towards us, frantically pushing debris out of her way, and screaming, "Where's Harry? Where's Harry?" over and over again. Her kids were crying. Their baby brother was missing. Their distraught shouts echoed around the dirty water.

'Dad must have him,' yelled the girl.

We helped their mother onto the balcony. Fear was etched on her face and her eyes were wide and startled as she held her kids tightly.

"Don't worry, I will find him," she said, hugging them and stroking their hair. They all stood together in silence. It seemed like an eternity. I stood nearby, feeling helpless. My fear seemed trivial in comparison. She looked anxiously out at the jungle.

"Don't worry, stay where you are, I will find him Harry, Harry!" she screamed.

The water was now right up to our balcony – about fourteen feet high. People, their clothes torn, were clinging onto the branches of trees. The Sri Lankan men, used to scaling them for coconuts, were much higher up than the westerners. They were shouting in Sinhalese to one another, from tree to tree, and although I couldn't understand them I realised that they were calling out the names of loved ones. "Ydavil, Ydavil", which means help, was another constant refrain.

I couldn't work out how so many people had ended up in the water and then it made sense. They had been on the beach and got swept along in the wave. It had all happened so fast. They were still wearing their swimwear.

We pulled more victims onto our balcony. Their bodies scraped against the rough concrete, adding to their injuries. Once safe, they screamed and shouted, begging us to find their loved ones. The fear that it wouldn't stop was the same for us all. There was utter devastation all around and tons of junk floating by. Luke, realising this was deadly serious, had started to think of ways out.

An Australian couple with their son scrambled onto our balcony. They were a mess. The woman kept screaming that their house had collapsed on top of them and a concrete wall had crushed her under water. They were bleeding quite heavily and had sustained nasty injuries. The only possession they had, apart from the clothes still hanging onto their battered bodies, was a surfboard.

Harry's mother asked for the surfboard, explaining that she wanted to search the water for her son. The Australian couple were traumatised and appeared reluctant to give her the board. At the time I thought this was strange, but later I understood their situation. If another wave came the board might save their lives.

"I need it!" she said, snatching the board from them, before jumping off the balcony in search of her husband and baby.

I watched as she leapt into the black water and laid on the surfboard, splashing frantically, calling out her husband's name, her cries echoing around the jungle and water. The two kids started crying, their lips trembling and teeth chattering. I remember thinking that I wouldn't have dived in, it was far too dangerous. But then I wasn't a mother and I could see that she had no care for her own life, only her child's. She quickly vanished out of sight.

Another man swam towards us. He had a bad injury to his right shoulder; the muscle was hanging off like a piece of meat at the butcher's shop. We helped him onto the balcony. He was in his fifties, had a dark, neatly-trimmed beard and moustache with flecks of grey. He said he was Tim, from Guernsey, and was anxious about having swallowed the water, mixed with sewage. Luke remembers thinking at that time, 'don't worry about that, we need to sort that wound out,' but Tim was in shock and frantic with worry.

All we had were antiseptic wipes, Germolene and our used bed sheets and towels – not ideal. I couldn't remember if we had a first aid kit to hand or whether it was with Fran. I couldn't look at Tim's wound from fear of fainting. I tried to talk to him to keep him conscious while Luke dressed his shoulder. His lips were trembling and he was very pale, his legs were shaking and he was nervously bouncing them. I thought he might pass out as his eyes kept rolling upwards, so I rubbed his hands to get his circulation going.

I tried to make conversation but he was shell-shocked. I learned that his wife was missing. Tim's eyes were empty as he told us that they had been on the beach, having breakfast, when the wave came. He had tried to hold on to his wife but they were torn apart. He had been tumbling in the water and when he surfaced he had lost her. He was terribly worried. His wife was recovering from a brain tumour and wouldn't be able to take her medicine. I felt helpless. I thought she must have drowned and there was nothing I could do.

He kept saying, "The corals are exposed," shaking his head, and "The bay is empty." I didn't understand but pretended that I did.

Tim's daughter was also missing. The poor man, I couldn't even begin to imagine what he was going through. I carried on rubbing his hands. They were shaking more than mine and this helped to calm me down. I remember calling out his wife's name with him.

"SANDRA, SANDRA," we yelled into the water, over and over again. No voice called back.

By this point we were completely surrounded by the ocean. We stood there in silence, too scared to talk. None of us could comfort one another. We all realised we were in trouble and no words would change that. I felt on the verge of hysteria. I jumped out of my skin again as another house collapsed into the water, splashing and sending ripples around us. People were still screaming and shouting but we couldn't see where they were.

Suddenly we all snapped back to our senses as the air was filled with a noise that I was to become only too familiar with over the next few days. Panic filled every nerve in my body. It was a noise that makes your blood run cold and freezes time. The sound of a mother whose child is dead – the woman who had left on the surfboard had found her baby. Baby harry was the first of many victims of the tsunami that we would see. I watched as the father swam in the water carrying the limp body of his beloved son, his wife behind them, and climbed out of the rancid water onto the opposite balcony. The baby's legs were dangling lifeless. The father looked dazed as he passed the infant to the mother and she held him close to her chest as if nothing else could hurt him. I could see her grief and hear her cries and felt sick with horror.

Her sobs filled the air. I watched speechless as people tried their hardest to resuscitate the infant. Hysteria and panic was terrifying. It was too late. I witnessed his mother accept his death with great dignity. She held him close to her chest and rocked his limp body, rubbing his back as if singing him to sleep, her head hung over him, her other hand extended as if to protect her husband.

In a surge of panic, her teenage kids jumped into the water and frantically swam towards their mother and father and baby brother, yelling and screaming, in the dirty water.

"Noooooo. Noooooo. Please no, dad, mum, noooooo." Their wails rang through my body.

They paced up and down the opposite balcony, gibbering and shaking, hitting the concrete banisters, and pleading with strangers to do something. The son was tearing at his red football shirt, pulling it over his face in grief, while their dad tried desperately to comfort him.

Baby Harry brought the reality of the situation coldly to light – this was really bad. We were in the midst of a natural disaster. A baby had died while on a Christmas break with his family. The family was ruined.

That moment was the most shocking of all and one that haunts me still. It just didn't seem real. I felt as though I wanted to wake up from a bad dream. Luke recalls how his heart sank at that point. The pain he felt was incredible and yet he was still trying to digest the seriousness of the situation, and was asking himself what were we going to do?

The daughter of the Australian couple with the surfboard had ended up on the roof of a house in front of ours that had also withstood the force of the wave. She shouted at us to help her. We couldn't understand what she was saying as there was so much noise. Then Luke realised that somebody was trapped inside the building. She was tearing at the tiles, throwing them into the dirty water.

Luke jumped over our balcony and, landing on the roof, ran towards her. He could hear the tiles cracking under his feet and didn't know if they would support him. I noticed that Dammika's dad's bungalow had collapsed and this house was similar, so could go at any time. Luke helped the girl rip the tiles off the roof. I saw Dammika standing on the opposite balcony looking out to the sea, but there was no sign of his family. The old man in his white vest was nowhere to be seen. His veranda had gone.

"What are you doing?" I selfishly shouted to Luke, "Come back, it might collapse," but he ignored me.

With their bare hands they made a hole in the roof big enough to fit a person through. I watched as Luke's top half disappeared as he leant in and pulled out a young Sri Lankan girl with the help of the Australian. She was traumatized, screaming, pulling at her log hair. She was about thirteen-years-old, with a slender frame. Her traditional dress was soaked and stuck to her body. Then Luke pulled another woman through the hole to safety. She was also hysterical. They had been trapped on the ground floor, in the water, and were terrified. How they had not drowned, I'll never know.

Luke helped them onto our balcony. The girl kept pointing towards the jungle, screaming and crying, and shaking my arms. Luke said it sounded like 'papa' but we weren't sure. She had a tiny splinter of wood or metal stuck in the white of her right eye and wanted me to remove it. She could barely open her eye and it was weeping badly. My hands were trembling so much that I couldn't do it. No words would comfort her because she couldn't understand me. I knew that the person she was trying to tell me about was probably dead so I just sat on the floor and held her tight. I rocked her and stroked her wet hair while she sobbed onto my shoulder and cupped her eye. It must have been agony. The other woman Luke had rescued sat on the floor with her face in her hands, gasping, and her grey wet hair, tied in a thick plait, stuck limply to her face. I looked over her shoulder at the water and saw the bodies of three men float by face down. I held back my scream for fear of causing hysteria.

One thought kept rearing its ugly head in my mind: Luke's family. It was too awful to contemplate. As I held the girl I prayed that they were OK. They were all on the ground floor and Zimmer Rest Guest House was further around the bay from us. Hopefully Thalik would have known what to do and had looked after them.

The air was strangely silent apart from the sobs and wailing of the bereaved and injured. Grief echoed around us. We were all paralysed by the thought of another wave. Playing a waiting game with Mother Nature, will she or won't she, each one of us helplessly awaiting our fate.

Then there was another loud noise; a whirling, groaning and sucking. I looked across to the people on the other balcony, facing the sea, watching their faces, looking for an answer. Terrified that another wave was approaching, we all began screaming. I let go of the young girl and grabbed the balcony rail waiting to be engulfed by water. Bracing myself to take on the power of the wave, knuckles white with pressure, I held on with all my might. I knew it was possible that the wave might go over us and I planned to try and get on top of it and swim. I don't remember anybody else around me at that point, not even Luke – it was every man or woman for themselves.

I stared out at the horizon, praying to be saved.

Then I noticed that the water level was starting to drop! I thought that my eyes were playing tricks on me, but they weren't – it really was going down. We all laughed nervously, strangers thrown together in this disaster, not sure what it all meant. The loud noise was the ocean sucking the wave back. It was receding, it was fucking going back! Some of us started to laugh. We were safe, for now. However, everyone who had survived the incoming wave would now be desperately fighting for their lives in the retreating water. We began to hear shouts and screams but could not see anyone. I just hoped that they were able to grab onto something as they were pulled along.

I suddenly recalled kayaking in the Ardeche in the south of France, when I had crashed into a rock on a fast-flowing, deep rapid. The kayak had flipped and I had found myself pressed against the rock with my head somehow stuck inside the space that you would normally sit in, the power of the water was like nothing I had experienced before, its force was incredible. Luke had vanished and I was sure he had drowned. I tried to escape, but the water was pinning me to the rock. Then something shifted. I was sucked out of the kayak and remember the rushing of the water filling my ear drums, before I bobbed up to the surface in my life jacket and caught my breath.

The accident happened next to a nudist beach. Two middle-aged naked Frenchmen had run to my rescue and pulled me onto the riverbank. One of them was wearing an Australian hat with corks dangling from it. I was sure Luke had drowned and was shouting his name until he appeared from behind a black rock, waving at me. I was crying, holding hands with the two naked men. The relief I had felt was indescribable. He, on the other hand, was baffled by what he saw. "Only you!" he said, as we thanked the men. They had retrieved our purple kayak from down river and we got back into it and headed off.

Now, I watched from our balcony in Sri Lanka as the ocean sucked everything backwards, the debris was crashing against anything in its path and the noise was overwhelming. Fear was still paralysing me – I didn't know what would happen next. But, for the moment, the water seemed to be dropping. I breathed deeply. On the horizon I saw the roof of a van appear, then a window. It definitely was dropping. I looked at Luke. He was staring motionless at the van too. Tim laughed nervously and pointed at the white vehicle as it slowly started to emerge from the water. I hoped it was empty and nobody had drowned in there, but it was too far away to see.

"It's... its dropping, the water is leaving, it really is," he said.

We laughed nervously and hugged one another. As the wave retreated, it revealed the devastating damage it had caused. The noise of the water had died down, but the commotion around us was unnerving as wails rang out; people screaming loved ones' names. Distraught, they stood chest-high in water, their clothes in tatters, holding their arms to the sky, shouting and sobbing, begging for somebody to help them. The terror in their eyes was heart breaking.

On our balcony, we were all talking too fast with different ideas racing around. We were traumatised and nothing made sense. I remember thinking that I really was probably going to die and that just because the water had gone for the moment didn't mean we were safe. We couldn't leave the balcony as we didn't know what might happen next. Rooted to the spot, in fear, I could feel my heart thumping in my chest, but all I could do was watch.

One thought kept returning in my mind: where was Luke's family? We had arranged to meet on the beach early this morning. I was imagining the worst. Zimmer Rest was quite a walk away from us. I just hoped that the wave hadn't reached them. I had no idea of the scale of the disaster and hoped it had been confined to our part of the bay. I prayed that, like us, they hadn't made it to the beach early, but their rooms were all on the ground floor. The structure of Zimmer Rest was very similar to that of the Village Inn, a sturdy concrete building. Maybe they had been able to climb onto the roof. We just didn't know. Pat and Fran were Buddhists and we were in a Buddhist land. Surely they would be helped?

In less than ten minutes the sea had roared across the land, spewing a giant wave over us, racing through the jungle and taking whatever it wanted. The power of the wave left little standing. It overturned ships and fishing boats before tearing inland. Unawatuna would never be the same again. The sleepy fishing village was gone. It had been devastated in minutes. Nobody could have prepared for this. No words of wisdom had been passed down through the generations. This was a freak accident.

Like me, the only thing on Luke's mind, other than dying, was his family. He had been thinking about them the whole time. He knew that this was a natural disaster after seeing the first body, and feared for his family. He needed to go in search of them. Village Inn was situated in a dip and the water was still deep in places. He stood in silence trying to find markers to judge how much the water was going down. Then I heard the words I had been dreading:

"I have to go and find mum and dad," he said, bluntly. I nodded.

I felt everything slow down. I knew Luke had to do this and that he had quite a walk ahead of him, but I also knew that I couldn't accompany him. My legs were like jelly and I would be a hindrance. I felt safer here but if another wave came, I could die. I cried.

It felt like we had been standing on the balcony for days. Luke tried to convince me that everything would be all right. He pointed to figures in the distance, walking among the trees where the water had receded, to reassure me he would be OK. I had to trust him. Luke realised he would have to wade through the water to his family. I could see him shudder at the thought of all the dead bodies in there, but his mind was made up and he went to find his sandals. He told me to wait for him and that he wouldn't be long. We didn't even kiss one another goodbye. I watched him walk down the steps, leaving the safety of our balcony, into the water. He stopped when it was waist high and then started to wade through the debris, his arms outstretched for balance. I watched Luke as he struggled through the water and held on to this last image of him, as if I might never see him again. Then he turned a corner and disappeared out of sight. I looked at the sea. I hated it. I prayed he would return safely to me. A lump rose in my throat and I tried to swallow. This was no time to cry. I was being selfish but my vision blurred as my eyes filled with tears; I couldn't stop them.

I knew Luke would be gone for some time as the walk normally took twenty minutes on the road. Now there was only water. I wished I had said more to him when he left; all I said was 'bye'. How strange that this was the only word we said to one another. Maybe it was because we thought that if we were casual, it would be OK. I suddenly felt very alone and cursed the fact that we hadn't brought our mobile phones to Sri Lanka.

"You shouldn't have let him go," a voice said, bringing me back to reality. "There will be a second wave."

I looked at Tim. I was mentally drained and couldn't even answer. The tears streamed down my face. An explosion made us all jump. It was the toilets exploding as their drains burst.

The next two hours were the longest of my life. My knees were knocking as I started to pack our rucksacks and I talked loudly to myself. It felt strange collecting our possessions together but I didn't know what else to do. I needed to stay busy. I felt lost without Luke there by my side. He always makes things right. I wasn't sure if I would ever see him again or be reunited with his family. I began to morbidly imagine my life without him, my partner and my best friend. I didn't know if I could go on if he died. I understood that he had to leave but I hated him for it too. What would I do now if another wave came? If I survived this disaster and Luke and his family didn't, I would have to return home on my own with all of them dead. It was unimaginable. Although there were people all around, not one of us was capable of comforting each other.

I had packed all of our stuff apart from our toiletries. I had to pluck up the courage to go into the bathroom. Its window faced out towards the sea. If a wave came I would see it and I wasn't feeling brave enough to look. I took a deep breath, as I pushed the door open and started to hum, "always look on the bright side of life, de der, de der, de der de der de der." There was a mess from the burst drains. The room stank and made me feel sick. I didn't dare look towards the window. 'Keep your head down, don't look up,' I muttered as I grabbed what I could, shoving the toiletries into my bag – such weird and trivial things to collect at this time, but they might be useful later. I returned to the balcony. Everyone was standing in silence, cut, battered and bleeding, trying to make sense of the situation.

I recalled our arrival in Unawatuna, all the happiness and laughter. The visitors' book still sat on the table untouched by this chaos. As I flicked through the pages, trying to lighten my mood, I thought about scribbling in the book 'tsunami'. I read again about how wonderful it was here, how peaceful and calm. This had been exchanged for the sounds of screaming and despair. It had become hell.

I walked up and down the balcony, feeling empty, as though I was looking at myself from somewhere else. I imagined the poor people who would have been swimming or snorkelling when the waters receded. They would have all died. This was a nightmare, an absolute fucking mess. I looked at the sky through the palms. It had been replaced by a dull grey instead of its usual clear blue. I held on tightly to the balcony. My legs were shaking and I felt almost drunk with fear.

I heard the chattering of a monkey and looked up. There I saw a toque macaque with his punky hairdo parted down the middle. He was dangling casually on the branch of a tall palm with his legs crossed. Peeling a tropical fruit, he looked me straight in the eyes, then at the dirty water below him. 'What the hell has happened?' was the puzzled expression on his face. He watched us all with curiosity and kept raising his eyebrows and flashing his teeth as if trying to communicate. He popped the fruit into his mouth and began chewing, still watching us feeble creatures on the balcony. Then he turned and bounced off through the palms that had withstood the force of the wave and vanished. Mesmerised by this animal, I had briefly removed myself from all the commotion.

I thought back to early hours and the figures in my room. It seemed like a lifetime ago. I wondered who they were and whether they were my guardian angels.

9 – LUKE'S LONELY WALK

I said goodbye to Tracey and walked down the steps of the balcony. The water was black and full of shit. I was wondering if it was even possible to get out of here at this point. I was apprehensive but didn't believe there would be another wave. I had done some work on tsunamis so maybe I had a false sense of security. Unfortunately I had only a little knowledge about these giant waves and, as the old saying goes, 'a little knowledge can be dangerous'. I thought the general rule of tsunamis was that they were triggered by one-off seismic events. As I later found out, this is not entirely true.

I stepped into the water and was shocked by its coldness. Before then, the sea had felt like a warm bath. I could feel my feet treading on things. I knew there would be glass, sharp objects and snakes in the water, even dead bodies. It reminded me of the scene from *Star Wars* when the main characters are trapped in a room full of dirty water with junk floating around them, not knowing what to expect. I was surrounded by tables, chairs, sun-beds and washing machines, all bobbing on the surface or partially submerged.

I looked around trying to focus on a route out. The only way was to trudge through the debris. I didn't know what I might find and thought that at any moment something might jump out at me. The Village Inn was in a dip, something I had not paid attention to before, nor needed to. All the paths had vanished; nothing was recognisable anymore. I was desperately trying to find a way out, just a rough path. But this was proving impossible.

I kept catching my feet on things and was glad I had worn my trainers instead of sandals. I was really aware of every step I took. One false move and that could be my end. I decided on a route, even though I didn't know where it would lead me. All the time I was desperate not to fall or slip. My heart was pounding, my lips were dry and my mind was full of images of my family. The walk to the main road, the Yadehimulla road, normally took a minute. Already I had been wading for at least fifteen minutes and seemed to be getting nowhere.

There were fish gasping for air. I wasn't sure if they were freshwater fish struggling in the marine environment or if there was just no oxygen in the water. They were making horrible noises as they flapped about fighting for their lives. It was unnerving.

Nobody else was trying to leave. I wondered if I was doing the right thing but the compulsion to find my family was immense. Absolutely desperate, I thought they might be dead, which filled me with a fear I had never experienced before.

I eventually came out onto higher ground. There were people standing on a large slope, obviously trying to digest the devastation that had happened in their village. I could just make out where the road had been and saw an internet café smashed to bits – only three concrete walls remained. It was where Tracey had called her family the day before. Two big hotels were badly damaged but still standing. I could use them as landmarks. I was starting to move more quickly now. The water had drained away in places but the debris was still an issue. I couldn't believe that such a small place could leave me feeling so lost.

In the distance I saw some Sri Lankan lads in their twenties climbing over things. This gave me hope – I wasn't alone. But suddenly I realised that I was at the sea! I had gone too far and needed to go back on myself. I was frustrated with myself for wasting precious time. I turned around trying to find my way but everything was unrecognisable. There was so much devastation I had no other markers. I stopped and tried to remember the way. Again, I worked out a route and just hoped it was right. It was a cruel game trying to find my family.

There were electric pylons strewn about in the water. I watched some Sri Lankan lads using the cables to pull themselves over the debris. I realised that the electricity was down so it was safe to copy them. I struggled in the hot sun, up and down over mounds, slipping and sliding but able to hang on. I kept thinking about my family and was becoming more and more frightened of what I would find. Their rooms were all on the ground floor of their hotel or they could have been on the beach.

I passed the hotel where we had all had dinner the night before and remembered how happy we'd all been. I wanted to cry but wouldn't let myself. The ground floor was destroyed but the concrete shell had withstood the wave. A wall that had run along the beach was now on its side. Three foot thick, it was like a running track. Suddenly, my brain registered this fact. I felt a surge of relief as I jumped onto it and started jogging. All I could hear was my heavy breathing and the sound of the sea. I was scared but determined. Sweat was running into my eyes, stinging them and blurring my vision, but I carried on running. My head was pounding from dehydration.

Fear churned in my stomach – what if my family was dead, how would I carry on without them? I imagined how scared they would have been. Please, please let them be all right. I started to notice that the damage wasn't as bad around here. Maybe, just maybe, they were alive. I carried on running, jumping up and down off the wall where it had split and smashed. My breath was laboured and I felt knackered.

Shops were still standing with clothes hanging from the ceiling. I started to smile as I ran. The tide marks around their walls were only about four or five feet high. Good. There was a poor bedraggled dog on a wall, soaked and whimpering in shock. It was probably dying. I wanted to stop and help but knew I had to keep going. I felt guilty and couldn't get him out of my mind as I ran.

I came around a corner and saw in the distance my mum and Nathan! There was no mistaking her mop of red curly hair. I started shouting and they turned around. I thought my eyes were playing tricks on me or that I had heatstroke. I squinted and put my hand to my brow to get a better look. It really was them, it really was. My soul instantly lifted. I started to run towards them and slipped, falling into a gutter at the side of the road. I felt the skin peel away from my legs as they grazed against its sides.

I was so exhausted I had no energy left and was in pain. A couple tried to help me to my feet but I was shattered. I slowly pulled myself up covered in the thick, slimy mud and realised that this was the least of my worries. How typical to slip over right at the end of my trek. I got to my feet and saw the blood from my fall but I didn't care. My family was alive.

10 – LUKE RETURNS

I heard Luke's voice shouting: "Trace, Trace."

I ran to the side of the balcony and saw them. Thank God! Luke was safe and was accompanied by Nathan. I was overwhelmed and started to laugh hysterically as my teeth chattered. But still I wondered had the rest of the family survived?

They were wading through the debris and I saw them lift out of the water the body of a young boy and place him on a door that was floating by. They gently pushed him away in the water. I studied their faces for clues, to see if they had all survived. Nathan looked up at me and gave a half-hearted wave of his fingers. I knew then that the rest of the family would be alive. Luke and Nathan appeared relatively calm and were both smiling at me.

"Get your stuff, we have to go. Hurry!" shouted Luke, as they ran up the steps to our balcony.

"Where is everybody else?" I asked.

"Safe, don't worry," said Luke. "Come on, get your stuff."

We all hugged. I felt guilty, having my family return in front of the bereaved on the balcony, but I also felt huge relief.

"Come on, we have to hurry, we've been told there's another big fucker on the way," said Luke.

"Oh no, please don't say that," I said.

Luke, finding his family alive, had calmed down. They were all in a state of shock but had quickly decided on a plan of action. Fran had told Nathan to accompany Luke to get me. Nathan told me that he froze. Once Fran had given him his orders all he felt was an intense fear. There was a long pause, but he knew he had to do as his mum said and leave with Luke. The rest of the family had arranged to follow Thalik to a monastery on a hill.

Luke and Nathan had said goodbye to their family and started the long and frightening walk back to the village to get me. They told me there was shock and devastation everywhere, but they were surprised to see people carrying bikes. Luke and Nathan had watched in wonder thinking, 'leave your bikes, save yourselves, not your bikes.' They found it surreal, like walking through a war zone. Injured and bereaved people wandered aimlessly, bleeding and crying, unable to comprehend what had happened. Luke and Nathan had been lost in their own thoughts when they were alerted by the screams of people:

"WAVE! WAVE!" "MORE WATER COMING!" They had run the rest of the way.

"We must leave now," said Luke getting impatient.

"Where to?" I asked. "Please don't make me leave," I begged.

The small balcony offered security and had saved our lives. The boys talked me through it. There was higher ground a short walk away where we would be safe from another wave. A place called The Rock. I was terrified and tried to persuade them to stay on the balcony, but Luke sternly told me to get my bag and leave. I knew by his eyes that it wasn't open to discussion. I had already wasted precious time.

Feeling vulnerable, in the hands of Mother Nature, we grabbed our stuff. Nothing had been damaged due to the height of our room. We walked down the steps into the water leaving the rest of the survivors on the balcony – I don't think we even said goodbye. I felt faint, a familiar feeling from my childhood after visits to the dentist for tooth extractions. Nathan carried my rucksack over his shoulder. The water was waist-high, cold and dark, and I began whimpering to myself.

It reminded me of when I had fallen into the hippo pool at the zoo one morning. I didn't know the whereabouts of Nicky Noo, the female pygmy hippo. Then I felt a thud against my leg and realised I was not alone. I panicked as I treaded water, knowing that my movements would unnerve her. She had bobbed up in front of me spraying my face with snot and water and I could feel her warm breath on my face. My heart racing, I spoke slowly to her:

"Hello Noo, how are you?" I asked.

Her whiskers twitched as she opened her huge mouthed. I could see her bright pink gums, sharp spiky canines and her big fat tongue rolling around inside her mouth. I could see steam rising off her body and the vapour of her breath. Her ears were rotating, spraying water droplets. Sweat beads formed on her nose. She took a deep breath and vanished underwater. Oh no! Where the hell was she? I managed to swim to the side of the pool and tried to crawl out but I kept slipping on the algae. Then I felt another thud on my back and she appeared to my right. I was cold, frightened and my radio was water damaged so I couldn't call for help. Noo started splashing around excitedly and winding herself up. I tried to talk to her and reached out to stroke her face but she snarled at me, menacingly. She took another deep breath and vanished into the murky water. I was in trouble. I felt a tug at my arm and she appeared again with my coat sleeve in her mouth. I pulled my arm away from her jaws, thinking, this was my lot, this was how it was all going to end…

"Trace!" I knew that voice! It was Alan my fellow keeper, thank God.

"Al, I need a hand, mate," I begged.

"Here, grab this." I managed to shake Nicky Noo off my arm and grabbed Alan's broom. He pulled me out of the water. I looked back at the hippo and could swear she was laughing, her head was thrown back and her huge pink mouth was open. It was a lucky escape.

Carrying our belongings, we started to wade through the mess. I took care not to tread on any sharp objects by gently testing the ground with my flip flops before putting my weight down. The water was horribly cold and black. Breathing deeply, my lips trembling, I was listening for the roar of the second wave. Then I lost one of my flip flops and freaked, unable to move. Nathan searched in the water and retrieved it. Normally placid, he was becoming impatient with my fear that I was so jittery and slapped it into my hand.

We walked towards a clearing. As I tripped over the roots of a tree, a young Sri Lankan man held out his hand to steady me. We were now in-between the Village Inn and higher ground. If a wave came now we were fucked – there was nowhere to go. We clasped hands and walked in silence, squelching through the mud, slipping and sliding, until we reached The Rock House. It looked untouched by the wave. As I walked up a steep pathway an overwhelming sense of calm filled my body and I savoured the comfort of dry dust under my feet.

11 – THE ROCK HOUSE

The Rock House was a set of small, neat apartments with balconies built into the hill. Everything looked untouched. Apart from the fear of the survivors you would think nothing had happened. We walked up a dusty track into the centre of the complex.

All around people were in shock. Loved ones were missing. Badly injured people were lying on the ground moaning and crying. It reminded me of scene from a war film. People were gradually realising the scale of the disaster. Crowds were gathering, speculating about what had happened. Others wandered around dazed. Rumours of more waves, much bigger than the last, were circulating. 'Fifty to a hundred metres,' I was told by one man. The Rock wasn't that high. We were doomed. 'There will be one at two o'clock,' someone else said. Would the next wave take us, or the one after that? Nobody knew. All we could do was sit and wait.

Every now and then people would start screaming, "WAVE, WAVE!"

Hysteria spread further up The Rock as people started to run, falling over themselves as they scrambled to get higher. This was the highest point in the village. We just had to hope the sea wouldn't take us. In many ways, the hours that passed that afternoon and the night that followed were more terrifying for me than when the tsunami actually occurred – then the panic had been instant. This time I was waiting for another wave and contemplating how long it would be until I died.

We found a shady spot to sit and collect our thoughts. The locals started handing out bottles of coke to drink. I took one and thanked the man. I swigged at the bottle but my hands were trembling and it was hard to keep a grip. My mouth was dry and my lips were cracked and I had difficulty swallowing. I watched as pandemonium unfolded around us. There was lots of shouting and arguing. I felt punch drunk.

A small, thin Sri Lankan man limped towards me crying. His feet were sore and bleeding. On closer inspection I could see his wounds were quite deep from walking barefoot. He was pointing at his toes then clutching his chest, tears rolling down his muddy face. He wanted me to help him. I nodded at him patting Luke's rucksack for him to sit on. I emptied my rucksack to find something – even soap would do – and discovered that we had our medical kit! I began to clean his wounds. The cuts were dirty so I used baby wipes to try and clean them up as best I could and smothered them in Germolene.

Every year, Luke and I have the same argument before going on our travels: why do I need so many pairs of shoes? I then have to sneak them into various compartments of our rucksacks. But on this holiday they proved to be one of the most important things I had with me. When I finished bandaging the man, he limped away wearing a pair of diamante flip flops from Accessorize. I never saw him again.

The Rock was slowly filling up with tourists and locals with various skills. I sat dazed in the hot sun watching all the commotion. A rumour went around that a doctor had arrived. Sian, a Welsh woman based in

Melbourne, was petite with short dark hair and a kind face. She was wearing a brown and orange Lycra swimsuit and shorts. We all got our medical kits together and she quickly selected various things to help her on her mission to make a doctor's bag. She was calm and professional as she began tending to the injured. She worked miracles given how little she had.

Sian's presence filled people with hope. I didn't see her stop working from the time I first clapped eyes on her until we left. Her kind, reassuring smile made us feel safe. Despite her own trauma, and with three young children who needed their mum, over the next few days she shared herself around anyone who needed her help.

Sian was joined by a stocky man in his fifties, wearing khaki shorts, a t-shirt and big army boots. From his accent, I gathered that he was from the north of England and guessed that either he had been, or was, in the army. He had tightly cropped, silver hair and stood very straight with a commanding presence. He was a great support, and although his deep, loud voice was very different from Sian's gentle manner they complemented each other very well.

He spoke bluntly to people about their injuries but gave a realistic diagnosis. I remember him telling Tim, the bloke with the torn shoulder muscle, that he was lucky to be alive as the cut had missed a main artery by only millimetres – if it had been any closer he would have bled to death. Sian and the army man worked hard, running to help people in need of their skills. I think everybody at The Rock that day will always remember them with the utmost respect. Many survivors might not have been so lucky without their help.

Stuart was an elderly gent in his mid-seventies. He had sustained some nasty injuries and swallowed a lot of rancid water. He was a sorry sight wrapped in bandages and unable to move. We approached him to try and keep up his spirits. We learned that he was a seasoned traveller and had taught English all over the world for forty odd years. Stuart had been having breakfast on the beach like so many others when the wave hit. He described how the bay had emptied after the first wave, exposing the sea bed with its spectacular rocks and corals. Fish could be seen flapping around on the rocks and sand. The bay had been empty for at least an hour before a wall of water came into sight at incredible speed, spilling into the bay and onto the land.

Stuart had been with his Egyptian friend, Haluk, who, sadly, was another victim of the tsunami, although he wasn't aware of this then. Sian had asked us not to tell him in case he went into shock. Stuart told us how he had been swept along in the torrent. He said it felt like a rugby scrum and he had covered his head with his hands, as he was hurled in and out of hotel rooms, and was battered by everything in his path. He had swallowed huge amounts of water. Luckily, someone had managed to help him to safety.

Sian had told him not to smoke but the crafty old monkey asked us for a light. He picked up his cigarettes with shaking hands, and put one between his trembling lips. He inhaled and smiled at us, sucking the smoke into his water-filled lungs. I heard him gurgle. He asked if I had any painkillers so I went and got some Nurofen and a bottle of water. Afterwards, someone told me that Sian had already given him some earlier and that too many painkillers could thin his blood and kill him in his weak condition. Shit! Had I murdered Stuart? I felt terrible and ran to ask Sian but she said he would be ok but shouldn't have any more. She raised her eyebrows when she saw Stuart smoking and looked at him disparagingly, but he just smiled. Luke told me to stop interfering.

Nathan spent a lot of time with Stuart listening to his tales, which helped take his mind off the constant fear of the wave and gave him something to concentrate on. He must have been in terrible pain but I never once heard him moan or complain, despite the severity of his injuries. The only thing he kept asking us was whether we had seen Haluk. We all lied to protect him.

Some of the Sri Lankans had started to make fires and were boiling water and cooking rice and dahl in the huge pots. A small self-sufficient village was beginning to take shape. Sian's children had been busy ripping up bed linen to use as bandages.

A western man had a small transmitter radio. The reception was poor but he told us that there had been a gigantic earthquake and the Maldives had gone. He held the radio close to his ear, concentrating with a worried frown on his face. I watched as his expressions changed, hoping to learn something new. Every now and again he would shout out a country and we would gasp, trying to make sense of the news.

Some Sri Lankan men gathered around a tuk-tuk, they had managed to rig up to a generator and listened to the news. Information was coming through of a huge earthquake in the ocean off Indonesia. Huge tidal waves had travelled through the Indian basin destroying vast parts of Asia.

Then we heard that Phi-Phi, in Thailand, was destroyed with thousands dead. Africa had been hit, AFRICA! This didn't make sense at all. We listened in silence as they translated the news to us. I felt confused, my heart was pumping and I thought I was going to faint. Everything slowed down. I started to realise the true horror of what had happened. We were in the middle of a natural disaster. It felt to me like the Apocalypse was here.

We didn't know what to believe, as far as we knew, anything was possible. In pidgin English, I asked one of the Sri Lankan men if England was OK. He shook his head and I burst into tears and ran to the man with the radio. He wouldn't answer me and gestured for me to go away, as he listened intently with a heavy frown. Luke told me I was being irrational and to stop bothering people with senseless questions.

Then, as threatened, the second wave came. People came running up to The Rock with fear in their eyes and there was renewed pandemonium.

"WATER, MORE WATER!" they screamed.

I started running with them. All I could hear was screaming and the sound of our feet pummelling the rocky track. Crowds of us were running to get to higher ground. I looked for Luke and Nathan but they were still with Stuart. I begged them to leave him and come with me but they refused. They insisted that the wave wouldn't reach us. I ran off on my own, crying, caked mud crumbling under my feet as I scrambled to get higher. I grabbed at roots to support myself, slipping on rocks, not daring to look back. I could feel the sun beating down on my forehead as I climbed. I started mumbling to myself. My lips were dry. I paused and a Sri Lankan woman offered me some water. I sat with her, both of us trembling, and unable to communicate for she spoke no English and I no Sinhalese. She held my hand.

Around us, I could see that people were badly injured. One young girl lay on a makeshift stretcher, her leg twisted and bent backwards. It was obviously broken and she wailed in pain. Lots of people had head injuries with bloodstained, makeshift bandages wrapped around them. Young, barefoot Sri Lankan men were carrying injured relatives in firemen's lifts over their shoulders.

Again, it was absolute chaos. A western woman began to hand out sweets to the children but most of them were too traumatised to take one. Everybody was in shock. I still felt selfishly angry at Luke and Nathan for staying with Stuart. He had lived his life, how could those young brothers stay with him? The only people I cared for when I heard "Water!" were those I loved. I had never thought I would feel like this but at that moment I was in survival mode.

Thankfully, I didn't actually see the second wave. Apparently it was the same depth as the first and once again it had unleashed its power on the village. Later, we were told that it was much more ferocious than the first.

Once the panic had subsided, some young local lads started to climb back down to The Rock so I followed and found Luke and Nathan still with Stuart. I felt ashamed about having left them, but Stuart smiled, so he evidently didn't hold it against me.

On the balcony of one of the apartments we got talking to three English lads. People's rooms lay empty with their personal belongings strewn across their beds as if they had popped out to have breakfast but had never returned – it was eerie. Paul was a northerner with a generous smile and a dry sense of humour. I liked him a lot. He tried to keep our flagging spirits up with his quick wit. Neil was intending to travel around the world for a couple of years, but this was the first leg of his trip. Andy was on holiday in Sri Lanka, but lived and taught English in Phuket in Thailand. His girlfriend was there. He looked terrible. He had survived the wave in Sri Lanka but had no way of finding out about her.

Paul had been staying at the Village Inn on the ground floor. We had exchanged pleasantries with him one morning when we were having our breakfast. He told us that on the morning of the tsunami he had heard roaring and then water had started pouring into his room. The previous night, he had locked his door and left his key on the bedside table, but when he looked he realised that it had been washed away and he couldn't get out. Panic set in as his room started to fill with water. He was pushed up to the ceiling with only a small space left for him to breath. He had thought this was the end but luckily the pressure of the water burst the bedroom door off its hinges. Taking a deep breath he had dived under the water and swam through the door and out. He had managed to climb onto the balcony opposite us.

Neil had a similar story. He too had been stuck in his room, but managed to swim to safety. Andy had been on his balcony and saw Neil in the water. At first, he had wondered what he was doing swimming around but quickly realised that he had escaped his room on the ground floor. He had helped Neil onto his balcony.

The Rock House was full of people wandering around, bleeding and crying. They kept stopping strangers to describe their children, babies, husbands, wives, brothers, sisters, aunts, uncles, girlfriends, boyfriends, mothers, fathers, nans, granddads or friends.

All MISSING.

Something I hadn't really thought about – or hadn't allowed myself to think about – was the dead. What would we do with them? How many people had lost their lives?

I looked down and saw Sunil, our friend from the restaurant. He was walking around looking dazed. He was wearing only his dhoti and his long hair was wet and tied back. He was crying. I ran down the stairs and called out to him. He turned around and we embraced. I held him tight as he sobbed into my ear. His beautiful baby son was missing.

He explained how he had managed to hold on to him as they were dragged along but when he slammed against a palm tree his son was ripped out of his arms. Frantic, he had gone after him but the water was too quick. He could see his baby boy but couldn't reach him in the ferocious waves.

He sobbed loudly and wailed, "MY BABY, MY BABY."

The despair in his eyes tore at my soul. I cried with him, before he left the safety of The Rock to search again for his baby. I had a bad feeling about his beautiful boy after having watched the English family find baby Harry dead. The wave was too powerful for small children who had been violently taken from the arms of their parents. I saw Helga, Sunil's wife, sitting on a balcony. Her feet were bandaged and she was staring into the distance. No words would help. I felt sick. What the hell had happened? I wanted to go and help Sunil look for his little boy but I was too terrified to venture down there. I watched him walk alone into the jungle, dragging his bare feet along the dusty ground, his shoulders shaking with sobs. He was a broken man. I remembered meeting his little boy, his cute haircut and ready smile.

So many people were missing and I was starting to realise that this probably meant they were dead. A Dutch couple in their thirties had lost their child as it was swept out of the father's arms in the same way Sunil had lost his child. The father was distraught, pacing around with a haunted look about him, his eyes red and swollen. I heard him explaining how his child had felt slippery, like a bar of soap, as he tried to hold on to her. Finally, the baby just slid from his grasp. These poor men were tormenting themselves for having lost their children. I knew how hard it would have been to hold onto somebody else, especially a baby, who couldn't hold on tightly to you. The tsunami had been like a huge washing machine swirling water around ferociously. I wanted to say something to try and comfort him but I just couldn't find the words. He was frantic. His wife was being comforted by an English woman in one of the apartments. I could hear her crying and wept for her.

They had two other boys with strawberry blond hair who looked forlorn and their eyes were soulless. They were so confused. Their toes were black with mud. I smiled at them, I didn't know what else to do, and they smiled back. They were playing a board game with three teenage girls but knew that something terrible had happened.

Then a familiar sound rang out. The same howling I had heard when baby Harry's mother had found him, my blood ran cold. I knew it was Sunil. He was carrying the limp body of his baby boy, his legs hanging loosely by his daddy's waist as if he was asleep. Sunil was cradling his baby's head and kissing him. I watched from the balcony with horror and a scream came out of my mouth before I could stop it. I hugged Nathan as we cried.

The little boy's mother's screams rang out. Her desperate wails made everybody stop what they were doing and stand in silence. We shouted for Sian the doctor and like a Mexican wave the next group of people called her, and the next, until she heard and came running. She tried her hardest to resuscitate the boy but it was too late. His poor mother kept repeating to Sian that his legs were still warm. She was desperately hanging on to any hope that he might come back to life, but of course it was too late. The warmth of his legs must have been from the sun beating down on him before his daddy had found him. The same beautiful little boy we had watched on Christmas Eve, in his white outfit, playing with his Christmas tree, showing us which lights he had chosen, was now dead.

A deep sense of sadness overwhelmed us. This was so cruel. I watched as

Sunil and his wife stroked his pale cheeks and body. His mother's long, slender fingers tidied his hair. They lay either side of him, their feet entwined, as if to protect him from danger and kissed and hugged him repeatedly. Everybody left them alone to grieve.

Before Sunil returned, Helga had shown me photos of them at a funfair a few weeks earlier. The happy family were smiling and waving at the camera. She held them close to her chest. They were unrecognisable now – torn apart. She touched her tummy and told me she was expecting another baby. Now, she sobbed and sobbed as I held her hand.

Similar screams rang out later that afternoon when some Sri Lankan men found the Dutch couple's child. I watched from afar as they gently washed the mud off her face and wrapped the child in a clean sheet ready for the mother. I recognised the little blonde girl from the beach. Her mouth was slightly open showing small white teeth. Days before, I had watched this child playing in the sand and had thought how pretty she was. The respect the local people showed the westerners was overwhelming. A local woman was cradling the child. She looked peacefully asleep. I watched them climb the steps to the apartment where the mother was waiting. Sobs burst from my chest and other people broke down as the child was carried past them. We all knew that behind the door a family was waiting for news. Now their worst nightmare would have come true and their lives would never be the same again.

As they approached the room, everyone fell silent. I saw someone open the door and then the air filled with wails. Everybody stopped what they were doing and hung their heads in a mark of respect for the family and their young daughter. I thought about the two little boys. How would they understand that their sister was dead? There was nothing anybody could do for this family but let them grieve in privacy. I never saw the little boys again.

The local men had received news that another 'tidal' had hit Hikkaduwa which was about thirty kilometres east along the coast. It was over 100 metres tall and had destroyed everything it in its wake. Apparently, it was heading here. My lips and legs began to tremble and I slid down the wall onto my knees. Like a cruel game of cat and mouse we awaited our fate. We panicked at every bang and crash. But an hour passed and we were still alive – the wave never came.

All afternoon, bodies were brought to a makeshift morgue. There seemed to be no end to this horror. As the evening drew in, the locals brought food and candles. There was no electricity. During the day, the tourists had joined them to go down to the beach and salvage whatever they could – crates of fizzy drinks and bottles of water washed up from the beach bars. After dinner we helped collect plates and washed up. Firewood was collected and chopped to keep the fires burning. Coconuts were cut down from the palms to drink and eat. Huge bunches of bananas were salvaged from the jungle and left on the balconies. People had retrieved mattresses and sheets from the hotel rooms that had withstood the waves.

"Look!" shouted a small child. We all jumped and turned around. She was pointing at a dark mass bouncing towards us. "MONKEYS!" she exclaimed.

We watched as a troupe of toque macaques arrived. These primates are always up to mischief and in true macaque style they were going to get whatever they could out of this disaster and nobody was going to stop them. They started trying to lever the windows off their hinges, bouncing around, shaking them, throwing things, jumping up and down in frustration, creating havoc.

One macaque was on look-out, flashing his teeth at the pasty-faced tourists and furiously moving his brows up and down as if to goad us, while others set about the burglary. They curiously examined tubes of sun lotion, towels, clothes, books, magazines and various other items, tossing them to the side when they realised that they weren't edible. We all watched and laughed – they lightened the mood, temporarily. The troupe left empty handed. They stomped off towards other apartments where the rattling and chattering started again. It reminded me of a scene from the TV series of Sinbad. Later, I learned that the last two episodes of the show had been filmed in Sri Lanka.

12 – THE NIGHT AFTER THE TSUNAMI

The evening bought the mosquitoes. They settled on our dirty, sweaty bodies. I remember the sound of everybody slapping their skin as they bit us all over. The buzzing sound of them around my ears was driving me insane. I scratched my legs until they bled. We had no mosquito repellent to keep them at bay. We were worried as we hadn't any Malaria tablets. I had taken Larrium tablets when I went to Northern Thailand and they had made me so ill with paranoia and hallucinations that I just stared out of my bedroom window, drooling. They made me so anxious I never took them again. I always just smother myself in jungle juice and hope for the best. But the mosquito repellent was with Fran at the monastery.

Further threatened waves never came. We had been told that the next one was due at 2.00am. I sat hunched against a wall, my mind playing havoc with me. Tidal waves had been my biggest fear ever since I had watched a film with my sister, as a child, about a huge wave devastating a city. I thought of Dawn. She would be mad with worry and, knowing about my phobia, she would probably imagine me dying in the same violent way that we had once watched as children. I tried to have happier thoughts but it just wouldn't work. I squeezed my knees tight to stop the trembling and rocked backwards and forward to comfort myself. Somehow, drowning in the dark seemed worse than during the day. I thought of the passengers on the doomed voyage of the Titanic. It must have been horrendous sinking in the freezing cold ocean in the middle of the night.

I watched a Sri Lankan woman approach Nathan. He looked so young and innocent. She tilted her head as if to apologise for what had happened. It was as though the local people felt somehow responsible. The night brought a feeling of unease as the darkness hung over the rock. If another wave came now we wouldn't stand a chance without any light. I watched the moon and wished I had the power to fast-forward time. It was eerie and strangely silent. All we could hear was the crashing of the ocean, as if it was teasing us with its power. There was also the menacing sound of corrugated iron roofs banging against the rocks. Normally, the nightlife would muffle the sound of the sea. At least the wave hadn't hit during the night, I thought. It would have taken many more lives in the busy beach bars.

The fruit bats, also known as flying foxes, began their nightly duties, blissfully unaware of the chaos beneath them. I watched their wings working hard to keep their fat little bodies in the air. They flew for short distances and would land on trees to feast. I watched them for ages and thought that if we had wings we could get to higher ground and then we would be safe.

I saw Dammika, the owner of The Village Inn, arrive with his family. He was beating his chest. His father, auntie and a brother had all died. The wave had rushed through the ground floor houses and taken them. No words would be of comfort to Dammika at this moment. His grief was too raw, but we hugged him anyway. He was such a proud man, he kept his emotions hidden. He had to be strong for the family that had survived.

They all looked so lost. I watched him from a distance as he continued to beat his chest with his fists.

We had been given a room by a German couple. They had fled to the hills after the first wave to stay with friends but had left their luggage behind. We decided to put Dammika's family in there for the night as they were deeply traumatized. His son with the bowl haircut had a tear stained face. I squeezed his hand and smiled at him but he didn't smile back this time. He looked haunted; an innocent soul, damaged. The young girl Luke had helped to safety through the roof turned out to be Dammika's niece. She was extremely upset and chattering to herself. Her eyes were hollow and one was still swollen. Dammika's brother came to thank Luke for saving his daughter.

"A thousand thank-yous my friend."

"No worries mate," Luke replied and shook his hand.

As the full moon fell upon The Rock we were all grateful for the light it gave us. I remember Dammika's brother pointing at the moon and saying:

"By day nature has been very bad but by night it has been good."

It amazed me how these people could still see the good in things when they had lost so much.

This was to be the longest night. We sat in silence a lot of the time, collecting our thoughts and trying to make sense of events while keeping one ear on the sound of the waves crashing. We were emotionally and mentally exhausted. I thought of how much I'd enjoyed hearing waves break on the seashore before the tsunami. I loved wrapping up and going for winter walks along English beaches, but I couldn't imagine doing that again.

The darkness made me feel vulnerable, even with the moonlight. Some people were able to snooze while others just paced around. I walked around in circles muttering to myself. Sobs could be heard throughout the night as people grieved, many of them alone. I could make out their shapes, hunched over or rocking.

I heard a persistent moaning. It reminded me of two separate occasions when two visitors had jumped into our Asiatic lion enclosure at the zoo. Arthur, the male, had attacked them both. The first time, a man had climbed into the enclosure to offer the lions some frozen chicken. A couple of years later, another visitor tried to re-enact a scene from the bible. Both men received nasty injuries but amazingly survived.

Arthur had not wanted the frozen chicken and had attacked the bloke almost immediately. He thrashed out at him, lifting him off the ground with one paw, engulfing his whole head in his jaws- much to our horror- as we tried to distract him. His pride watched from afar, unsure of what this strange man was doing in their home. Arthur, his mane standing on end, shook the man like a rag doll and he looked tiny by comparison. It was like some horrible scene from a film set in Roman times. We stood by helpless as Arthur dropped him to the ground with a thud. He lay motionless. Then Arthur dragged him by his head into the centre of the enclosure. We all craned our necks to see if the man was still breathing. Arthur dropped him again and began licking the back of his head. As the man moved, we all shrieked. Arthur slammed his huge paw onto the man's back to stop him from moving; the keepers were calling him back he suddenly abruptly walked off back to his lair and into his den to feast on a donkey's leg. The man was alive, his moaning could be heard across the enclosure. Later, he was taken away by ambulance.

The second man's biblical act lasted less than two seconds. He was shouting words from the bible he had clutched in his hand as Arthur attacked him. Again, he dropped the man to the ground like a discarded toy, before ripping his chest to tatters, while two cubs each grabbed a leg. The lioness sat back watching them, flicking her tail excitedly and growling. Arthur left the man on the ground and lay close by watching his prey. I sat on the other side of the fence, not daring to move, breathing heavily. I could see his golden coat trembling, his tail swooshing backwards and forwards, and his nostrils opening and shutting; his big pink tongue licking his lips, his eyes slanted and his nose twitching. He shook his mane, waiting for the man to move one more time, ready to pounce and finish him off. I was so close, my knees shaking, talking to this stranger as he moaned loudly. I was pretending that everything was ok in order to keep him conscious and calm as the blood ran from his body onto the grass. I thought he would die right there.

"Don't move," I whispered, as he groaned pitifully.

He must have been in agony; his black skin lacerated with deep pink slashes. The keepers tried to get the lions into their den by calling their names. Finally, Arthur returned inside followed by his pride. The paramedics arrived on bikes and I sat on the ground, my heart thumping, as I watched them working on the man. He was also lucky to leave in an ambulance and not a coffin.

I followed the sounds of moaning and found an old Sri Lankan man behind a boulder, comforting his daughter who had Down's syndrome. She looked scared but was not injured from what I could see. I smiled softly at the old man and he nodded back, looking tired and fragile. I asked if he needed any help, but he shook his head so I left them alone. I wandered around the camp. It was humid and quiet. The small fires shed light on a pile of dead bodies lying by a tree covered by towels.

Luke, remembering that we had a box of wine in our room at the Village Inn, had slunk off without telling me. He returned beaming from ear to ear. I was furious with him for going when it was so dangerous. We found glasses and cups and shared it around. Dammika stayed and drank wine with us. He was mostly silent, lost in his thoughts. Now and then he looked up with raised eyebrows and sad eyes and simply shook his head. All we could do was be with him. The alcohol helped to calm us until Andy pointed to the image on the Californian wine box. It was of a palm tree next to a lapping ocean. Before the tsunami this would have been an inviting image, but now we all shuddered. Huddled together under the moonlight we sipped our wine and whispered together.

I desperately needed to get a message home to my family. I knew how worried they would be but all communications were down. There were no phones and no internet. I had asked people with mobiles if I could phone my family but they had all said no. I could understand that they were worried that their batteries would soon run down with nowhere to re-charge them. Paul, the northern lad, tried to make me feel better by saying that although our families had not heard from us yet when they did they would be relieved, unlike so many other poor families who would be receiving the worst news of their lives. He was right of course but I just wanted to save mine the worry. I hoped that at that point they weren't aware of the scale of the disaster.

In the early hours I met Linda, her husband Dave, and their three teenage daughters. Linda had received a text from her brother in England updating her with information he had read on the internet. He had told them to try and get home soon as there might be more earthquakes. We sat and chatted and Linda offered to send a text for us. I was overwhelmed until I realized that the only number I knew by heart was Luke's. All my numbers were stored in my phone sitting on our kitchen table in London. I ran to wake Luke and he thought he might be able to recall his friend Andy's number. He returned with me but as he started to give Linda the number his mind suddenly went blank. There was nothing we could do but go with what Luke remembered. She sent our message: 'WE ARE ALIVE. CALL TRACEY'S MUM VIA DALE'. We just had to hope that he would get it. Dale is a dear friend of mine who has phone numbers for my family. Hopefully this would make sense to Andy.

I sat with Linda and smoked a cigarette. She had a very soothing voice although I knew that she was as scared as me. Her daughters were trying to get some sleep. She told me how one of her daughter's had been working in an orphanage in Colombo and the rest of the family had decided to come over for Christmas to spend it with her. They had also been looking forward to a tropical Christmas. Her daughter hadn't been enjoying her time at the orphanage very much and she thought the tsunami would give her a good reason to return to school in England. Linda told me she had comforted the Dutch mother while she waited for news of her child. The girls I had seen playing with the Dutch couple's two boys were Linda's daughters. They had become friends on the beach.

Luke and Nathan slept for a few hours. I kept watch, too terrified to sleep in case I didn't hear another wave approaching. It felt like an eternity sitting there. Uncertain of what the morning would bring, my teeth kept chattering and my legs were trembling. The air was humid and sweat was running down my back. I wished that I could have a shower.

Yesterday, the sea had been the Sri Lankan peoples' friend; today it had become their enemy. The sea was everything to them, their provider. Now they were terrified and this showed on their faces as they wandered around the camp. I sat and watched them stop and exchange brief conversations with one another before walking away aimlessly. The only things they had left were the clothes they were standing up in. Some were lucky enough to be clutching the hand of somebody they loved, others stood alone. I had never seen so many grown men crying in my life; not even at a funeral had I seen such grief as I was witnessing here. I started to think about how many people in their village would be gone forever. The village was so small that they might have lost half of their community, maybe more. Earlier, somebody had estimated that maybe two to five hundred local people and fifteen to twenty tourists were missing.

Next to The Village Inn the small wooden shops selling fabrics and vegetables had been flattened. Those friendly traders, whose faces I would recognise, weren't on The Rock. Every night when we went out for dinner they had all smiled and said hello, their little shops dimly lit by flickering candles. They would have been open first thing in the morning at exactly the time the waves had hit. One old man ran a small Aladdin's cave selling anything and everything. It was the size of one of our garden sheds in England but rammed full with all sorts of things. He had a very distinctive white beard. I looked around but could see no sign of him, or of any of the other beach traders. I thought of the old man with his maracas. I had vowed to buy a pair off him before I left but now I would never have the chance. He could barely walk on his wooden stick; he wouldn't have stood a chance. I remembered the last time I had seen him limping away from us in the sand and felt very sad. I told Luke that all the local people were missing. He went for a stroll around the camp and returned to tell me that the waiters from The Hot Rock, the beach bar, had survived. They were in shock and bruised, but alive.

He pointed at two of the lads, with grazes and cuts on their faces, and we waved enthusiastically to one another. It seemed to be mostly young Sri Lankan men that had survived. Age and sex were evidently a factor. They looked different now, with tense postures and agitated faces. These lads from the beach bar would have taken the full brunt of the wave and by some miracle they had fought for their lives and lived to tell the story.

Overnight the Sri Lankan people kept the fires going, boiling water and handing out candles. A small group of men sat huddled around their radio, listening for news. I watched the light from the fire flickering on their desperate faces. They never slept. Twice they began to argue loudly and this sent a surge of hysteria around the camp. We did not understand what they were shouting about and people were frightened. Westerners started to yell at them to shut up. We never found out what it was about, but at least it wasn't the arrival of another wave. Other men spoke about all of the fishing boats that had been destroyed. One old man by the fire cried and kept shaking his head. Their lives had been turned upside down in minutes.

Four o'clock in the morning came and went with no sign of another wave. Again, I walked around our camp thinking of home, my family and friends and our new kittens Mindy and Frank. Who would look after them if we died? Who would have to sort it all out? I kept imagining my poor family going to our home, not knowing where to begin. We had no wills drawn up and the adverts on telly about life insurance kept running around in my head. During the last phone call home I hadn't passed on my love to all those people who make my life complete. How I wished I'd not taken them for granted. If a bigger wave came they would never know how much I loved them all. What a mess. I wondered if I could find a pen and paper. I could put a note in a plastic bottle for my family and friends. If I died, one day somebody would find it and have the addresses to send it on. Then I thought that I might be tempting fate.

How would it feel to drown? Quick, I hoped. I remembered an old friend of mine, Sandy from New Zealand, telling us about her white water rafting experience when she had been thrown out of the boat and sucked underneath the water. Twice people grabbed at her unsuccessfully and the third time she went under she said she felt very calm. She was so exhausted she didn't want to fight anymore. Surrendering to death was easier than the fight. I hoped it would be like that if my time was up. What worried me was my untimely death ruining the lives of those who loved me.

I had experienced this myself. In 2001, I was working with a tight-knit team in the Elephant and Rhino House when a colleague of mine, Jim Robson, was attacked and killed by one of our Asian elephants. Jim had worked at the Zoo for twenty-four years and it was his life. He was forty-four-years-old when he died.

It was a Sunday afternoon and we had just finished our lunch. Jim went off to prepare the elephants' lunch and I went to feed the hippos.

"Do you want a hand Trace?" he asked.

"No thanks. I'm ok." I replied

That was the last thing I ever said to him. Twenty minutes later a visitor came running towards me screaming:

"An elephant's killing the keeper! Please come, please come. You've got to do something!"

I knew by the look in his eyes that this was no joke. The awful thing is that I had often morbidly imagined what would happen if an elephant attacked a keeper. I dropped my broom and ran towards the paddock, radioing my boss who was at lunch. My legs were like lead. Visitors were running towards me in shock, screaming, trying to get away from the grisly scene. I tripped and fell over. Hauling myself up I could hear the female elephants. Jim was on the ground. My heart raced. I couldn't believe my eyes. There was blood everywhere and Jim was not moving.

"Pitchit, Pitchit, Mya, Geetha, Azizah!"

They stopped and looked at me as I jumped into the moat surrounding the enclosure. The elephants followed me. I could see Jim was in an awful way. His head was bleeding and he wasn't moving. There was so much blood. He needed help urgently.

I radioed the Zoo Gate Keeper, "Ambulance, ambulance now, to the elephant paddock. Keeper attacked!" I shouted. Other keepers were ushering the crowd away from the area.

The elephants were roaring and spinning around in shock, but we got them into their house and locked the doors. The Paramedics arrived on motorbikes and worked on Jim in the paddock. I ran over but stopped in horror a metre away. My legs started to buckle and I turned and ran to the staff mess room. I was sick in the bin and thought I was going to faint. I was praying out loud but I knew deep down that I would not talk to Jim again. Ambulances arrived with their sirens blaring. The rhinos were charging around, disturbed by all the noise, so I went to calm them down. I could hear a loud thumping sound. A helicopter had landed in Regent's Park to take Jim to hospital. The paramedics continued to work on him in the paddock, before lifting him onto a stretcher. His blood had stained the sand. I remember asking the men for their names as I thought Jim would like to thank them when he got better. They just smiled and nodded but didn't say anything. My friend Mandy was covered in blood and her face was ashen. I helped her to wash her hands under the hose. We were both in shock.

Two hours later, our Curator came to the mess room and broke the news that Jim had died from his injuries at the Royal Free Hospital and that the police were on their way to his family's home in Ulverston, Cumbria, to break the news. Everything was a blur. We all sat in silence trying to digest what had happened.

I rang my mum, in case she had seen the news, to tell her it wasn't me. I was in total shock. I was told to go and hose down the paddock to wash away all the blood. Without question I went, crying all the time, until another colleague came and took over.

I returned to the staff house, thinking that I would sort out Jim's locker. In frenzy I started to organize his things, ensuring that it was all in boxes neatly packed for his family, talking to myself for comfort. There were hundreds of photos of us all in the paddock with the elephants, doing shows, and walking in the Zoo grounds. Hot summer days spent showering the rhinos. Smart in our zoo uniforms, we looked young and carefree. I sobbed as I filed them away. I took a few to keep for myself. I folded his shirts and trousers and packed his jacket and walking boots. I washed up his teacup and put that into a box as well.

From that moment, I realized, nothing was going to be the same again. Only one month earlier, Jim and I had sat talking in the mess room about the Twin Towers in New York and wondering how the people that had jumped from the building after the planes had hit must have felt the moment they realised their lives were over. Six weeks later and Jim had faced his own mortality.

His violent death was to torment my waking and sleeping hours. I couldn't forget the sight of him hurt and dying. I kept asking myself if we have done more, if we could have prevented it. If I had said yes when he had offered to help, he would have been with the hippos and not the elephants. What did he feel just before he died? I know that he had had time to be scared because he was screaming. He knew what was happening and tried to get away but we weren't there to help him. He was alone and with no chance in hell of surviving the wrath of a four ton elephant.

What was it like to die? I spent the next three years trapped in this bubble of horror, with flashbacks constantly jumping into my head. Reliving that day, again and again, the image of Jim was always at the front of my mind. I dreamt about him every night for months, waking in a sweat, unsure if it had really happened. I wondered if he would look all broken if he came to me as a ghost. I became frightened by my own mortality, worried that everybody I knew and loved was going to die in an accident. If the phone rang late in the evening I would freeze, expecting the worst. I thought I would never be the same again as the months of grieving turned into years. As soon as the autumn leaves are on the trees, gold, red and orange, the skies are bright blue, and crispy frost is on the ground, I am transported back to the memory of Jim's last day.

For thousands of people worldwide, Boxing Day would now have the same impact as autumn for me.

I knew that if I died in a tidal wave then this is what my family and friends had ahead of them. They would spend their lives wondering if I had suffered, was it quick, and was I alone. It might have been a swift death but

I would never be able to tell them this, nor be able to comfort them. There would be questions with no answers and every Christmas would be a horrible anniversary for them.

I worried about Luke, if he survived and I didn't. He's a much stronger swimmer than me. How would he be without me? I never go out of my depth in the sea. The thought of drowning in this big salty monster was sickening.

I kept exploring every possible scenario over and over, consumed by my own horrors. How long could I hold my breath underwater? I couldn't think; seconds, or minutes? I remembered as a youngster panicking after jumping into the deep end of the local swimming baths. Gasping for air, I could hear the loud echoes of people having fun. I remember my eyes stinging, the breathlessness, the coughing and spluttering and then the sudden realisation that I was alright as my friend and sister appeared laughing at me. How long had that been? Probably, only seconds. I remembered *The Poseidon Adventure*. How long did the woman hold her breath under water…?

I shook away these morbid thoughts and walked over to check on Stuart. He was dozing. I covered his feet with sheets to stop the mosquitoes biting him. He opened his eyes and winked at me. I asked if he needed a drink and he nodded. I lifted the water to his dry lips and he took a few large mouthfuls. I plumped up his pillows to make him more comfortable.

How strange that I was helping the very man I was ready to leave to the waves a few hours earlier. He couldn't lie down due to the water in his lungs, so he sat in his chair, his chest rattling as he breathed. I didn't think he would survive the night.

"Thank you Florence Nightingale," he said, and we both giggled.

"Have you seen Haluk?" he asked

"No." I smiled at him, trying to look reassuring.

People kept an eye on Stuart throughout the night, checking that he was still breathing as they passed to use the toilet. An hour later, Nathan asked if I help to re-do Stuart's head bandage as it had slipped. I tried hard not to gag at the smell of rotten flesh and gently teased the bandage away from the pus. I used TCP and some ripped up sheets to dress his injuries, surprising myself by doing a half-decent job. He didn't moan and only winced a little. We tried to reassure him that his wounds were ok, but they looked awful. We covered his legs and arms again to protect him from the mosquitoes.

People were lying on the ground, restless, but attempting to sleep. I climbed over them trying not to disturb anyone. A couple had arrived who I hadn't seen earlier. A woman in a swimsuit was crawling along the ground. Her legs looked raw from what I could make out in the moonlight. She lay down next to her partner, a tall, slim man who was moaning in pain.

A colleague at work had given me a torch for Christmas. As I used it to go to the toilet I imagined everyone at the zoo going about their daily chores, laughing, teasing and chatting with one another, blissfully unaware of the terrifying situation that I was in.

The pygmy hippos, Thug and Nicky Noo, would be either having their swim or chomping on clover. The Bactrian camels, Nina, Nadia and Noeime, would be showing off their lovely winter coats all thick and fluffy- one blonde, two brunettes- to the gasps of excited children. The bearded pigs would be busy snuffling through the mud looking for their food, stopping occasionally to chase one another around their enclosure. Lucifer the lion would be impressing the visitors with his loud roar; the king of the zoo with his golden mane. The gorillas would be grumbling whilst eating their freshly prepared breakfast of fruit and veg. Zaire, our oldest gorilla, would be slurping her Actimel and grumbling with delight as she scraped the last dregs of the sticky fluid out of the plastic bottle, sure not to leave a drop. I missed them all. How I wished I was there right now in the safety of my job at the Zoo, our animal village in the middle of Regent's Park.

I would rather have my hands down a blocked hippo pool any day of the week. If I survived this, I vowed that I would never moan about my early morning starts again. I remembered my friends and colleagues seeing me off, taunting me about leaving them to work over Christmas. How elated I had felt, handing my keys in to the gate keeper at the zoo. This was my first Christmas off in fourteen years and I would be away from work for three whole weeks. I had waited all year for this holiday, waving off everybody else on their holidays over the summer months.

I wished I was home.

13 – MUM'S STORY

I was happily preparing lunch in the kitchen listening to Christmas carols as I peeled the sprouts. I heard the phone ringing and knew it would be Tracey phoning from Sri Lanka to wish us a merry Christmas. I picked up the phone and sure enough it was her.

"Happy Christmas Mum," she said, sounding upbeat.

The connection wasn't that good, the line was quite crackly, but it was lovely to hear her cheery voice.

"Happy Christmas my darling," I replied.

"It's beautiful here, Mum, we are on the southern tip of Sri Lanka on the beach. It's ideal. I think I prefer it to Thailand and India."

"Wonderful! I'm glad you're enjoying yourself."

"Are Dawn and Richard there yet?" she asked.

"No, not yet my love."

"Ooh that's a shame, you must tell her I'm on the most beautiful beach she will be sooo jealous," she said, laughing.

We chatted for a while and all too soon the minutes had gone.

"Give everybody my love and have a happy Christmas, I'll be thinking of you, I love you." she said, in a rush.

"I love you too; have a smashing time and love to Luke and his family."

"I will Mum. Take care; love you, bye, bye, bye!"

"Bye bye, my love."

It was great to hear her voice and I wished she were here.

Dawn and Richard arrived about ten minutes later and Dawn was sorry to have missed Tracey's phone call. We had a lovely Christmas Day and ate far too much as usual. It had been snowing and Dawn pointed out that although Tracey was on a tropical beach she loved the snow and would be gutted to have missed it.

They left at about 10.30pm that evening. I stood with my husband John and waved them goodbye. The snow was coming down quite heavily and the children in the street were all wrapped up in their winter clothes. It looked beautiful; like a fairy tale. I watched the headlights pick up the big snowflakes as they pulled off the drive.

We went inside and started to tidy up the aftermath of the festivities. I remember I started to feel strange and had an upset stomach, but put it down to over-indulging.

"Go to bed and get a good night's sleep, you'll feel better in the morning," said John.

I had a restless night and kept waking up in hot sweats, tossing and turning, and feeling really ill. Sri Lanka is six hours ahead so when the tsunami hit it was 3.20am at home. I was awake, unable to sleep, exhausted and on edge.

In the morning, at about 7.30, John got up and told me to stay in bed and get some rest. I was still feeling awful, so decided it was probably for the best. He went downstairs and returned with a drink for me. He looked anxious.

"What's the matter?"

"I think you had better come downstairs and watch the news. There has been an earthquake." He said.

I went downstairs and into the lounge where the television was on. The first images I saw were of a massive tidal wave and then I heard the commentator reeling off the countries affected – Thailand, Sumatra, Indonesia and Sri Lanka. Oh my God!

How can I explain the feeling that swept through me at that second? I think that I screamed. I remember rocking backwards and forwards.

"Not my Tracey," I cried. "Please God, not my Tracey."

John held me and said that it wouldn't be where Tracey and Luke were staying. He tried to convince me that they would be inland, high up, watching the sea as it swept everything away in its path. I knew that this was not true. I had spoken to Tracey yesterday. They were on a beach. They were on a bloody beach. Horrified, I watched images of the disaster unfolding. I wondered how Tracey, Luke and the rest of the family could possibly survive this.

I am extremely close to both of my girls and often know when they are going to phone but suddenly I had no way of reaching out to Tracey, in my mind or heart, or feel her reaching out to me. It was like nothing I have ever experienced. I just felt that I had lost her forever. I would never hear her cheery voice or smell Paloma Picasso as I hugged her; I would never touch her again.

My knees began to tremble and I was shaking and sobbing. John tried to reassure me.

"Luke is strong, he will look after Tracey. He won't let anything happen to her."

I knew this was true but how could Luke fight this disaster? I thought about Dawn. She was going to visit Richard's family in Sheffield and I asked John to phone and tell them the news. It would be best for Richard to decide how best to break this to Dawn. I knew she would become hysterical as my daughters are very close. They share a fear of tidal waves because of a film they'd watched when they were young.

When Dawn rang back we were unable to talk and just sobbed down the phone to one another. We tried to reassure each other that everything would be OK but of course neither of us truly believed it. We went over and over the possibilities and where Tracey, and Luke and his family might be. All we knew was that they were on a beach on the south coast which had been hit. We finished our call, too distressed to carry on.

More horrific footage was shown on the TV and huge numbers of dead were announced. I felt sick. A number came up on the screen for relatives to enquire about loved ones in the affected areas. So began the first call of many to the Foreign Office. I couldn't get through but finally Dawn did. She called to tell me that there was no news and we cried again.

I showered and dressed in tears. I went downstairs and started to clean the kitchen which was already spotless. I needed to occupy my mind. I scrubbed and scrubbed. John and I were trying to stay positive and kept reassuring each other that they were ok, but I had this dreadful feeling that I would never see Tracey again. I've asked myself time and time again why I felt this so strongly but I have no answer. Thank God my feelings were wrong.

The day continued with phone calls back and forth to Dawn and Richard. We were trying to be brave for each other but we were all distraught. Why hadn't Tracey called? When her colleague Jim was killed by an elephant at the zoo, Tracey had telephoned me straight away to save me any unnecessary anguish. This just added to my fear that something terrible had happened to her. I was frantic with worry.

John's daughter, Jayne, popped in to see us during the afternoon and I tried my utmost to be positive but the hours kept ticking by with no phone call. I talked with Jayne, trying to put on a brave face so as not to distress her, but I felt as though I was falling to pieces.

The hours dragged by. Some of Tracey's friends rang me from London and Birmingham to ask where they were in Sri Lanka and if I had heard anything. They were all very concerned. I could only repeat that I would let them know when I heard anything. It was difficult talking to people as it brought home to me the danger that they were in, if they were still alive.

All day I sat watching the television from the sofa. I felt so alone. I needed to know what was happening out there and hoped that I might spot them. It was soul-destroying to watch the devastation unfold but I needed to see it.

At about seven that evening the phone rang. I jumped out of my skin, expecting the dreaded phone call from the police. To my relief it was Dawn. She shouted down the phone:

"They're safe, Mum. They're safe. They're alive!"

Andy, one of their friends from London, had called her. He had received a text saying that Luke and Tracey were safe and to let me know. Relief washed over me. We were crying again but this time they were tears of joy.

When I was calmer I rang my sister Audrey and her husband Brian in Coventry to let them know that Tracey and Luke were alive. She had her family visiting for the day so they had been blissfully unaware of the disaster unfolding in Asia. I then rang my brother Donald and his wife Maureen in Herefordshire. They also had visitors and were completely shocked by it all. That only left my younger sister Lynda who had left for Egypt that morning and so I was hoping that she hadn't heard the news either.

John and I continued to feel shell-shocked, so we poured ourselves a drink and tried to unwind. I started to worry about Luke's family. The text had said that Tracey and Luke were safe but made no mention of the rest of them. Luke's mum has a sister but all I knew was that her name was Roz. I didn't know her surname, where she lived or how to contact her. How ridiculous to have no telephone numbers for Luke's family.

I went to bed very troubled and couldn't sleep. This was to be a pattern until they returned safely. In the early hours I went downstairs and sat in front of the television to watch the news. It was twenty-four hour coverage. I sat transfixed and horrified by what I saw. After a day or two John couldn't watch it anymore, it was too upsetting but I just sat there for hours on end, glued to the screen.

Monday morning eventually arrived. Despite my relief that they were both alive my fears about their safety were such that I could not stop crying. I couldn't speak to or see anyone. It was as if I was trying to build a protective shell around myself where no bad news could penetrate. John spoke to friends and family on my behalf. The only person I would speak to was Dawn.

On Tuesday afternoon I was in bed feeling awful when the phone went and I heard John shout:

"Tracey, oh my God!"

My heart stopped. He came rushing upstairs with the phone. Her usual cheery voice was full of anguish.

"Don't talk Mum; just listen, in case we get cut off. We're all fine, we're all safe. It's been an absolute nightmare but we are OK. Luke has been so brave and we have tried to help as much as we can. We are going into the hills to a retreat for a while to let the chaos calm down. Pat and Fran are with the doctor, having their feet treated, and we have food and water. Don't worry about us. Just pray for the people out here who have lost absolutely everything and everyone."

Then she had to go, saying, "I love you Mum, all my love to John, Dawn and Richard." I told her that we loved her too and to send love to the rest of Luke's family. I phoned Dawn immediately. We screamed with happiness. John and I sobbed and hugged each other with relief at hearing Tracey's voice but I knew that I wouldn't believe that they were really safe until they were back in England.

Fran's sister, Roz, had been frantically trying to find a way to contact us. She had rung London Zoo and tried to get hold of my number. She was put through to various departments and tried to explain that she needed Tracey's family's phone number. The staff had promised to try and find out something for her. For three days she rang and got the same answers. In the end she got through to the children's zoo and left a message on their answer phone. Fortunately, Tracey's friend Vanessa works there and heard the message. She immediately rang Roz and left my home number on her answer machine, and then called me with Roz's number.

It was so nice to talk to her and a real relief to share our anguish. We were both mad with worry. We talked for ages; two strangers sharing our innermost pain. It was strange that I didn't want to talk to anybody else but I could talk to Roz whom I have never met.

Roz's entire family was in Sri Lanka. She had despaired when the news broke and had been beside herself with grief. Although Roz had heard the day after me that they were all alive she was still feeling dreadful and unable to stop crying. She said she would not be able to relax until they were home. I agreed. I found a huge comfort in sharing my feelings with Roz and I had started to feel guilty for crying all the time. Our lovely family had survived. We should be feeling happy, but we didn't.

It was hard to fully comprehend the scale of the disaster. Although we obviously cared for our own, the images of the whole tragedy were deeply disturbing. Roz and I stayed in touch over the following days and tried to keep one another sane with long chats. We felt the same anxiety and shared the same fears of another earthquake hitting Sri Lanka while they were still out there. There was talk all the time about the risk of disease spreading. We heard that Sri Lanka had floods. The threat of more waves was reported in the newspapers. What if they had survived the tsunami but the worst was yet to come? Our minds acted on overdrive. I wished that they had their mobiles with them so that we could be in contact daily, but they didn't.

Roz told me that she was unable to go shopping or concentrate on anything except the news bulletins. Her twins, seven-year-old Lauren and Kieran, had been very supportive throughout it all. They had had to describe their cousins' tattoos and piercings for Roz to give to the Foreign Office as identification. She couldn't remember them herself. They had said that Tracey would have pink nail varnish on her toenails! They had obviously paid attention to such details.

On Saturday morning Dawn and Richard came to visit. We hadn't seen one another since Christmas Day and were chatting in the conservatory about the week's events when the phone rang. It was Tracey! It was wonderful to hear her voice and she sounded a lot better. Not her usual cheery self, but calmer. She reassured me that they were inland, in Kandy, far away from the sea. They had left Colombo as they wouldn't be able to get on a flight. It was pandemonium and they were going to wait. I passed her over to Dawn who sat back in her chair with the receiver pressed to her ear. Tracey was making her laugh and, despite everything she had been through, there was a twinkle back in Dawn's eyes. I watched and thought to myself – life goes on, how very lucky we are.

After the phone call we chatted about Tracey's description of the disaster; the sound of the wave, its aftermath, the dead people and the traumatised children. She told us that Luke and his brother had helped dig a grave for the bodies and that she had been too terrified to help at first. She sounded upset by this, but I told her that it was normal because she was in shock. Eventually, she told us, she had plucked up the courage to help the local women wrap up the dead bodies. It sounded awful. I was proud of them. I knew they would have done all they could to help.

The next day Tracey rang again to say they were coming home. They had managed to get their flights brought forward. I was thrilled. I couldn't wait to see them. All the time they had been away I really didn't know if perhaps they really were injured and didn't want to tell us. Finally, I would see for myself.

Picture Sigiriya – Camille, me, Luke, Fran, Nathan, Pat after the tsunami

Picture Elephant Orphanage – Pinnawala Back – Luke, Saskia, Fran, Pat, and Front – Nathan, me, Duncan (after Tsunami)

Picture Dambulla, Golden Temple.

After the Tsunami. Left – Nathan, Front Left – Pat, Front Right – Duncan, Right – Camille, Right Back – Fran, Middle – Luke

Picture Unawatuna 2004 - Tsunami Aftermath

The clear up with digger

Debris everywhere

Internet café with no windows where I had called home to wish them a
Happy Christmas

Picture Smashed Up Tuk Tuk

Pat outside his dads office in the middle of the tea plantation

14 – THE DOGS

The night's stillness was abruptly shattered by the sound of dogs barking. They were fighting. Everybody was very jumpy and any loud noise was traumatic. The growling went on for long periods and put us all on edge. Because of my shock, I had been dazed throughout the day and of little use to anybody. This was my chance to help. The dogs were worrying people.

I went down to the kitchen where a group of Sri Lankan women were sitting and chatting. I tried to explain that the dogs needed water by pretending to be a dog. I barked and made lapping gestures at a bowl in order to demonstrate that some water would calm them down. A German man looked at me as if I was mad.

"There is water everywhere!"

I looked him in the eyes and responded, quietly, "Yes, you're right, but it is salt water and no good to man or beast!"

He glared back at me but didn't hang around to help me take out the water that the women had prepared for the now rabid looking dogs. My plan was to put down the bowl and walk away calmly. I recognised some of the dogs from the beach as they were still wearing their neck-a-chiefs.

One was Sunil's dog, 'Chocolate'. He was usually very soppy and chilled. He was always looking for a scratch behind the ears and had sat patiently under the tables in the restaurant waiting for any scraps to fall to the floor. He looked very different now as he flashed his pearly white teeth. He was still wearing his little red neck-a-chief that had been tied lovingly around his neck by Sunil. I hoped that he remembered me. The young women were waiting for me to put down the water and watching my every move. I smiled at them trying to look confident.

I suddenly realised that I had put myself in a very stupid situation but I couldn't back down now. I armed myself with a piece of wood hoping that my rabies jab, supplied by the zoo, would protect me if I was bitten. I picked up a bowl and thought to myself: They're only dogs, I'm not scared. It felt like the first time I had entered the elephants' enclosure at the zoo, a knee trembling moment.

"Good boys," I said in my sternest voice, "It's alright."

I was trying to convince myself and not them. GGRRRRRR. I walked towards them and put the bowl down, pushing it with my stick. Four dogs came straight over, lapping furiously at the fresh water, making it spill over the edges. Don't waste it I thought. I felt a pull on my top and turned round to see a woman with three more bowls. I forced a smile and stuck my thumb up, pretending that I knew what I was doing.

"Nandri," I said, which means thank you.

I placed the other bowls on the dusty ground while the Sri Lankan men by the fire watched with amusement. The other dogs approached and they too lapped away. Soon the dogs started to wag their tails. I watched them and felt happy for the first time since Christmas Day. If only they could talk. At what time did they leave the beach? Where did they go? How long before the tsunami arrived did they know it was coming? If only they could have warned us of the danger, so many lives would have been saved. There was not one scratch on any of them. The women gave me some boiled rice which they devoured happily and their wagging continued. The dogs settled down quietly. I felt pleased to have been of some help. The women's beaming smiles told me that they were happy. People were traumatised and the last thing we needed was a pack of thirsty dogs on the rampage.

I returned to the balcony and watched Luke and Nathan sleeping. I was worried about Pat, Fran, Camille, Duncan and Saskia. We knew they had gone up the hill to a monastery with Thalik but I just hoped that they had stayed there and not gone back down to the village into the second wave. We had heard rumours of people returning to their hotels to try and find passports and various things only to run into the next wave and not be seen again. Hopefully Fran would have pulled rank and not allowed anybody to leave their safe place. I dozed off for a while, sitting in a chair, but at the slightest sound I would abruptly wake and jump up. I would then look around, see that we were alright, and realise that it was only a dream.

15 – THE DAY AFTER THE TSUNAMI

The dawn crept up on us with a chorus of discordant cries from the jungle. The birds were singing and the monkeys were calling to one another. I felt such relief to see the daylight and instantly felt better although I was still slightly deranged due to lack of sleep. People started to mill around exchanging pleasantries. The new day brought a different mood; a time to start organising and sorting. I looked over the balcony and could see that the Sri Lankan women had refilled the dogs' bowls and they were now resting quietly in the shade.

Two English blokes approached me clutching a pen and a piece of paper. They explained that they needed names and passport numbers to give to The British High Commission. We filled in our names and I remember my hands shaking as I scribbled down my details. Please let this information get back home, I thought, as I passed back the paper.

The Sri Lankans had prepared hot rice and dahl with bottled water for everybody. Hot cups of sugary tea were passed around. I remember wondering what would happen to these kind people if we got out. They were sharing all the food they had. What if there was no Aid on its way – what would they eat and drink then?

The Rock's well had been untouched by the tsunami so there was enough water to go around but this would run out eventually. When people had arrived, covered in raw sewage, they had headed straight to the well to wash. Thankfully someone had the forethought to stop this and to monitor the use of water. Separate washing-up bowls were set aside to bathe hands and feet. There was one for washing plates and cups and another with disinfectant to bathe wounds. A stout Australian woman had taken control of the well, guarding it with her life, and barking out orders to us all. Dressed in her bathing suit and walking sandals, a stern frown and her hands on her hips, she was a formidable taskmaster.

The Rock had become a self-sufficient village. The air smelled of garlic from the dhal bubbling away in huge pots, and an elderly Sri Lankan woman crouched beside them and stirred. I sat on a crate remembering Jim and that horrible day at the zoo. I recognised the same sense of trauma. I was frowning and my foot was tapping all the time. Anxiety filled my head and I felt only despair. My concentration was shot and I couldn't even string a sentence together let alone have a conversation with anyone. I was poised to jump up and run at any moment. I felt something like panic building up inside me.

Everywhere I looked people had the same vague expressions as if they weren't really there –

Tear- stained and heartbroken. People walked around, unable to make sense of it all. Some would have to return home with family members dead or missing. One young woman had a strange vine mark around her midriff. It looked as though a plant had literally grabbed hold of her and squeezed with all its might, like a huge triffid. She couldn't walk and was stuck in a chair with her legs supported. She had lost her husband and was in shock.

We sat in a small group, where we felt safe, trying to make stupid jokes to take our minds off things.

I remember Paul saying, "Hey Trace you're looking good. Been to a salon this morning?" We all laughed.

Luke still had the cat book I had given him for Christmas. He pulled it out of his rucksack and entertained us by reading out passages on over the top cat care.

Later, I looked in a bathroom mirror inside one of the deserted apartments. I smiled to myself when I realized what Paul had meant. Black mascara was smudged around my eyes and down my cheeks, reminding me of Alice Cooper, and my hair looked as though I had back-combed it for a fancy dress party. I found some cream on the shelf to wipe my face, ran my fingers though my hair and sprayed some aftershave under my arms. There was a slight improvement in my appearance. The toilets were revolting as they wouldn't flush.

The woman I had seen the night before crawling on the ground was now awake. She looked in pain. She had cuts on her face, her arms and legs were bruised and she couldn't move very well. She told me her name was Patricia. I had found a pineapple and she offered to cut it up for us, arranging the segments beautifully as though we were in some smart restaurant. Patricia told us she had been having breakfast on the beach with her friend when all of a sudden a wave rushed in, knocking over all the sun loungers and tables. People were desperately trying to grab their belongings when the next thing they knew was that they were being dragged along in a wall of water. She watched them as they were churned over and over in the mud and debris. She was heading towards two smashed-up cars when the water caught her and dragged her back into a house. She smashed against fridges and tables, before being sucked into another house. She was ready to surrender to death when the concrete wall behind her exploded saving her life. She managed to cling on to a piece of debris covered in leeches, giant millipedes and cockroaches before finding safety.

Her story was similar to that of other survivors with identical injuries. They had been slammed into the sides of houses and dragged along concrete walls. Sian the doctor came and treated her wounds. The most important thing was to keep them clean because of the polluted water and tropical climate – the fear of infection and disease was high. Patricia winced as her cuts were cleaned.

A pale, red-haired woman in her thirties, dressed only in her swimming costume, was shouting for a pair of trousers. I had some in my rucksack so dug them out for her. She put them on and walked away without even a thank you. She looked in terrible shock and her eyes were bulging like a startled hare.

Luke and Nathan had been asked if they would go and help dig a big grave. I was terrified that they would get hurt. Rumours of more waves came with the new day. For the second time I found myself saying goodbye to Luke and praying that he would be safe. All the men gathered what tools they had and left The Rock. I watched them walk to the road, turn right and out of view. I felt sorry for them and guilty too. I could have joined them. I'm strong and all I've done at the zoo for years is dig.

"If I was able to, I would be down there helping," said Patricia, in rather an accusatory way.

She made me feel bad. I told her that I was too scared and she rolled her eyes at me so I walked away. She was probably right. All my limbs still worked and I didn't have a single scratch on me. I took some deep breaths, got myself together and walked down to the makeshift morgue. Tearful Sri Lankan women were cutting up white plastic sheeting and collecting bed linen ready for the arrival of the bodies. I took another deep breath. I had seen Jim's injured body at the zoo. This final image of him had caused me great distress and given me nightmares for months, so I wasn't keen to deal with dead bodies, but Patricia had provoked something in me. There was a strong smell of disinfectant and a young girl scrubbed the floor. I approached a woman and took one end of the white plastic sheet so that she could cut along it. She touched my hand and nodded as she accepted my help. There were already a few bodies wrapped in sheets. I thought that this would be an easy place to start as I couldn't see their faces. The women talked to one another as they worked and softly chanted together. It was comforting to listen to them pray.

Out of the corner of my eye, I saw a group of people carrying the body of a young woman to the morgue. The men were upset and throwing their arms around. I gathered that they all knew her. Apart from the mud on her face, she looked as though she was sleeping. I wanted to vomit and felt my mouth fill with water. I swallowed. The overwhelming sadness was awful. I cried as I tried to imagine what she had been doing yesterday, before the wave took her life. She wore a wedding ring so was somebody's wife and maybe a mother. They folded her hands together on her chest and I watched as they wrapped her in a sheet, so that I would know how to do the next one. Her face was already swollen and a bluish colour. I felt as if I was intruding on their private grief, but then someone passed the end of a plastic sheet as if to confirm that I should stay.

The men returned, sunburnt and tired, ready to take bodies to the grave. Nathan told me how frightened he had been whilst digging, as all he could hear in the background were waves breaking on the shore. He kept one ear open all the time in case the pattern changed. It might give them enough time to run. They all had mental notes in their heads of what they would do if a wave came and which tree to climb. He told me how he had accidentally hit a Sri Lankan man in the head with his shovel because he was digging so furiously and we laughed.

The humidity was unbearable and a horrible smell began to fill the air. The corpses were starting to decompose. The bodies kept coming. There was lots of shouting and orders being given. Too many chiefs, too many opinions, I thought. It was unnerving. I waited, keeping out of all of the arguments.

Jamie and Claire, a couple from Brighton, in their thirties, had a digital camera with them, and Jamie bravely took photos of the deceased for identification later. The men started to collect old beds and doors to carry the bodies down to the grave. They picked up the covered corpses and gently placed them on the doors. They wrapped cloth soaked in Olbas oil around their faces to protect them from the smell of decaying bodies. Fear of disease had increased because of the heat, so it was important for the burials to take place sooner rather than later. I was joined by Claire. She was petite with short blond hair and a delicate face. We watched the men carry the bodies away. We were very proud of them, especially our boys, Luke and Jamie. Claire said she hadn't realized that Jamie had it in him. I agreed, but I had always known that Luke would help anybody.

Luke had been involved in an awful road accident in Malawi in Africa after the truck he had been travelling in burst a tyre whilst speeding along a dusty road. It had crashed killing almost all on board, bar him and a few others. He had cheated death as he had been sitting at the back of the truck, but was badly injured. I think he always felt guilty that he had not been able to help his fellow travellers. I think this was his way of laying those ghosts to rest.

I followed the men down to the mass grave. The old road looked as if a bomb had gone off. There was rubble everywhere and cars and boats were upside down in amongst the palm trees. Concrete walls were on their side, corrugated sheets were piled high and there was broken glass and rubbish everywhere. I saw a child's shoe lying on its own in the mud. I wondered who it had belonged to. I would never know, but prayed they were ok. People stood around in tattered clothes, confusion etched on their faces.

A monk dressed in beautiful orange robes had come down from the monastery to say prayers by the graveside. He looked as if he was finding it hard to make sense of what had happened. He too looked lost. Poor Luke was nominated to climb into the grave so that the bodies could be lowered down to him. I could see him go pale as he couldn't help standing on some of the bodies already in the hole. They lowered them in one by one. The bodies were heavy and Luke struggled and slipped as he worked. The monk chanted quietly.

It was surreal to see all these bodies being carried around. Everyone had a job but they were desperately trying not to think about what they were doing. As the body of a young woman was carried down into the clearing, there was lots of shouting and we all stopped in our tracks. A young man pulled back the sheet covering her face and let out a wail. He threw his arms to the heavens shouting and crying. Her eyes were closed and her lips were slightly parted. She looked like she was sleeping. Her hair was still plaited neatly. She wore a traditional bottle-green dress. Her face was slightly swollen but not as much as others I'd seen. She must have been in the shade when they had found her as she wasn't as decomposed as some of the other bodies.

The man who had wailed was her husband. He indicated that he didn't want her placed in the mass grave and preferred to bury her himself. He was shouting, crying and hitting his chest while arguing with the men carrying his wife towards the hole. It was clear that he was distressed and getting angry. He wanted to take her body with him and, of course, this was his right. I suddenly felt very bad for the survivors. Who were we, to be involved in this decision? It was unimaginable that somebody would do this to our loved ones back home. This made me stop and think about what we were doing. It was all so rushed and the local people who had lost family members were too traumatised to think straight. It was awful but we had no choice. We had been told that this is what we had to do if we didn't want to get cholera or typhoid. After a while, a group of young lads, also with injuries, approached the man and helped him carry his beautiful wife to somewhere more personal. I listened to his sobs as they faded into the distance.

In amongst the carnage, my eyes suddenly became aware of bodies tangled in the foliage. Some local men beckoned to me and Paul. They pointed to a body twisted in a plastic fence amongst jungle plants. At first we didn't understand what they wanted. The body was face down in the mud. The men rubbed the skin on their arms and shook their heads. Then it dawned on me that they thought the corpse might be that of a westerner. Paul leant down and scratched at the mud on a stiff arm and exposed brown skin. It was the body of a local man. He looked so pitiful on his own, the fence wrapped around his legs. He must have drowned when he got dragged through the plants. I morbidly imagined him panicking in the foliage, thrashing around and twisting backwards and forwards, trying to escape the weight of the heavy wall of water, until he could hold his breath no more. I stood silently. When he had awoken first thing yesterday morning he would never have imagined what his fate would be. The men started to untangle him. There was no need for us to hang around and see more horrors so we turned and walked away. There were various species of fish in the mud glistening as the sun reflected off them. The fish had been spat out by the wave and some still flapped about in shallow pools of water. I suppose we should have caught them and taken them back to the sea but it was too scary to think of returning to the beach.

I began to head back to The Rock sliding around in the mud trying to avoid any sharp objects. It was incredible that everything man-made had been destroyed but the palm trees had withstood the power of the waves. Once upon a time the beach would have had mangrove swamps lining its edges. These are chopped back to make the beaches bigger and to accommodate more apartments and restaurants. The mangroves grow in thickets along tropical coastlines. They have very complicated root systems which help to bind the shore together. This means they can provide an effective shield against destructive waves and act as a shock absorber. Up to half the world's mangrove swamps have disappeared in the last twenty to thirty years because of the development of tourist resorts and commercial prawn fishing. Mangrove swamps, had they still have existed, would have helped to slow down the force of the waves naturally. They would have saved lives.

I saw the Dutch couple coming towards me as they followed a Sri Lankan man. The father was carrying the body of their little daughter, wrapped in a red towel, two pale legs poking out at the end. Their faces ripped at my heart. Their complexions were ashen and they had swollen eyes and tear stained cheeks. They were still in shock and completely broken. No words seemed appropriate so I shook my head as they looked at me. The mother was bare foot and asked if she could have my sandals to go and bury her child. I gave them to her and squeezed her hand. I watched them head off in the direction of the mass grave. They looked like two lost children in need of their own parents. The grave site was very disturbing and I wondered how they would deal with leaving their precious child alone in this large hole full of dead strangers. They vanished out of sight.

I began to worry about not having my shoes. I looked down at my feet and could see mud and sewage squeezing between my toes and painted pink toenails. I started to walk, carefully, trying not to tread on anything sharp, but I was sliding around trying desperately to keep my balance so as not to fall over in this filth.

When I got back to The Rock, I approached the stern Australian bouncer at the well to ask if I could wash my feet. She gave me a bowl. The water was filthy but better than nothing. I rubbed my feet on the dusty ground to dry them. I went and looked for Luke but couldn't find him because he had gone to wash in the sea.

Luke is like a naughty child, always wandering off without telling me and causing great distress. When he returned, tears were rolling down his face. I was so glad to see him. Later, he told me he had been filled with rage and shouted at the ocean: "YOU FUCKING BASTARD! HOW COULD YOU HAVE DONE THIS?"

Luke suggested we should go for a walk together down to the beach to help calm me down. I reluctantly agreed. I took another pair of shoes from my rucksack and put them on. Hands clutched, we left The Rock and walked down the slope. I was terrified by the sound of waves breaking. Every footstep I took, I looked around for an escape route. My legs were like jelly and I felt really weak. To the left of us was the internet café where I had called my mum on Christmas night. All that was left of it was a concrete shell. The walls had been blown out from the back and the big glass windows were gone. It was full of huge pieces of broken concrete and debris. A young couple had run the place and they were always open in the morning. I guessed that they were now dead. It was difficult walking along, knowing all that was gone. Luke put his arm around me.

"Tracey?" a voice yelled, and I spun around. It was Berry, a friend of mine from England. Oh my God, was this whole thing a dream?

She scrambled up a small bank of mud with a huge grin on her face. I laughed out loud as we ran towards each other and hugged, laughing and crying, trying to digest if this was for real.

"There's been a fucking huge earthquake, Trace," she said, as if unsurprised to see me there.

"I know, off Sumatra we were told." I replied.

"Hope the orangutans are ok."

I laughed, trying to lighten the situation, looking at her in disbelief. Had I died?

Berry was washing her belongings in a small stream. She looked very shaken, but chatted away as she rinsed her things. She had actually been in the wave and survived. I watched her and thought how odd it was to meet here of all places.

Berry had been the Head Keeper of Rhinos at Port Lympne Zoo in Kent for twenty years and I had been the rhino Keeper at London Zoo for twelve. We had met at rhino conferences and both sat nervously together waiting to give our talks, clapping loudly after one another for moral support.

We became friends by drinking wine and eating chocolate into the early hours and talking about our passion for rhinos. My beloved black rhino, Jos, was moved to Berry's zoo and she had cared for him after me. This had been a wrench. Berry had helped me a lot after Jim's death at the zoo as she had been in the same situation two years previously. Darren, an elephant keeper at Port Lympne, was attacked and killed by Le Petite, an Asian elephant there. Berry had been one of the first on the scene as I had with Jim, but it had been too late. She had spent years agonizing about whether she could have got there earlier. Like me, she wondered whether if she had asked for his help it might have saved him. It sometimes felt like we were meant to meet through our rhinos and to be there for one another in the future. We would spend hours over bottles of wine counselling one another and trying to make sense of these terrible tragedies. Just to talk had helped us to accept the horrors of what we had seen and I was always grateful for our private chats. I think it helped us both come to terms with what had happened.

Berry had handed in her notice at Port Lympne Zoo to embark on her dream trip around the world for a couple of years, travelling mostly through Africa, working on projects with her beloved rhinos. She was the last person I had expected to see here. I never imagined that we would be brought together in the middle of a natural disaster. There should have been so much to catch up on but we weren't thinking straight. We just kept grinning and shaking our heads. Then I told Berry about The Rock and we promised to meet later.

"Be careful," she said.

"You too mate." We hugged and went our separate ways.

I looked at our once beautiful golden beach and stood in silence. I could not believe that it had all disappeared. The bars, the restaurants, the crystal blue sea. All replaced with debris, fallen electricity pylons, concrete slabs, smashed houses and cars upside down in the trees. A middle-aged man sat on an upside down beer crate with his head in his hands. All that remained was the odd concrete wall that had withstood the power of the wave. The sea was no longer inviting but threatening.

"I want to go back," I said to Luke, my vision blurring, and we walked back in silence.

A big yellow digger had arrived to start clearing the road. We were told that a wealthy Dutch man from Unawatuna had paid for it. Two young lads were driving this machine, steaming along, swinging a bucket around, and paying no attention to the safety of those around them. They were trying to make a pathway through the debris and were clearly enjoying themselves, grinning from ear to ear. I wasn't so sure that they had driven one before. Nathan hollered as the bucket just missed a Sri Lankan man's head. Best get out of the way, we thought. We had survived the tsunami and were not about to get killed by a digger. They were doing a grand job clearing the main road in Unawatuna, the Yadehimulla Road, which would make the village accessible to help from outside.

16 – LUKE'S FAMILY'S STORY

Camille had got up early the morning of the tsunami, which was unusual as she loves her sleep. Thalik asked Fran why Camille looked so anxious. She was pacing around smoking with a worried expression on her face. Fran agreed that Camille seemed nervous and told him that she had had a strange night herself. She had woken to see a cat staring at her from under the eaves. She had never seen this animal before and it had unnerved her. But she had managed to go back to sleep. When Camille sat down she said she felt on edge but shrugged it off.

Thalik told them he'd been on the beach early to practice his yoga and a single shallow wave had rushed up over his feet and then vanished as quickly as it had arrived. He was intrigued as he'd never witnessed anything like this in all his years of living by the sea.

Everybody, except Duncan, was up and they ordered breakfast. They sat on the verandah drinking coffee and tea. Pat's egg hoppers, a traditional Sri Lankan breakfast of fried eggs in pancakes with curry, had arrived. He was happy to be back in Sri Lanka and they were all soaking up the atmosphere. Suddenly, they heard lots of screaming. Surprised, they stood up to see people running, a tractor speeding past, and a van reversing right behind it.

"What's happening?" Pat asked Thalik.

"A fight in the village last week the army came and hassled the local women and a big fight broke out," he replied.

Then they saw the water and their first thought was that it was a burst water main.

"It must be from the sea!" said Thalik, surprised.

They were relaxed at that point, bewildered but not scared, as the water was shallow and not that menacing. But Camille had gone to the toilet and, seeing water gushing through the gardens, she ran back to the front to warn the others.

"Run! There's a flood!" she yelled.

Panic set in and they knew that something bad was happening when they saw how quickly the water was getting deeper. They all climbed onto the wall that surrounded Zimmer Rest and clung onto the edges of roof. Pat tried to grab a woman that had fallen over and was nearly taken away too. Suddenly, they realised that Duncan was missing. He was still in bed. They held on as the water kept rising. The sea was now roaring and the sound was drowning out everything else. If the walls of the house collapsed they would be swept away, but they had to get Duncan out.

For Pat, jumping into the water at chest height was a frightening prospect, but there was no other option. His son was in that room and he needed to help him. He motioned to Nathan to follow and they both dropped into the water and started to wade through the floating furniture towards Duncan's room. Their progress was slow as they had to cling to the walls and concrete pillars so as not to be washed away. Piled against Duncan's door was a mass of heavy furniture which they had to break through in order to force the bedroom door open.

Duncan had woken up confused and hung over. He had thought the local Sri Lankans were having a water fight in the gardens until it started to pour through the window.

"Come on!" yelled Pat.

"What's going on?" Duncan was still dazed and unable to take in what was happening around him.

"Don't know. But move your arse!" shouted Pat.

They grabbed hold of Duncan and pulled him along with them back to the rest of the family on the wall.

Some German tourists were now on the roof above them. Luke's family watched in horror as their baby suddenly fell face down into the torrent before bobbing back up. They all screamed and tried to catch the baby, whilst holding onto the roof themselves. Camille managed to grab its arm only for it to slip from her hands. Everybody was panicking. Camille jumped into the water and swam over to the infant. She held onto the baby for dear life. It was blissfully unaware of what was happening and made no sound at all. Camille managed to scramble to safety and passed the child to the parents on the roof. Nobody above seemed to register what she had done and how close they were to losing their baby. Had Camille not acted so quickly their child would have been another victim of the wave.

Fran saw the cat that had woken her in the night leap off the roof and disappear as it got dragged underneath the wave. Then the water stopped and everything went eerily calm. In the distance, they could hear screams and cries.

They noticed Thalik, crouching under the eaves of the roof, looking at the ocean. They stayed where they were while they decided what to do next. It was hard to make any rational decisions. A loud roaring noise made everybody scream as the water started to drop. The wave was being sucked back out to the ocean.

As the water receded, Thalik took charge and told everybody to collect their passports and to prepare to leave immediately. There was utter chaos. Cars and furniture were visible, strewn through the jungle. The family went to try and find their passports. As they waded through the mud, water and debris back to their rooms to see what they could salvage, they listened for the sound of more waves. They had to climb over piles of broken furniture to reach the entrance hall. Thalik guided them so as to avoid broken glass and they carefully moved aside planks with nails sticking out of them. All of his treasures, his beautifully carved furniture and the masks he was so proud of, were ruined.

Duncan and Nathan's room looked like a tornado had ripped through it and they quickly realised that they would be unable to salvage anything. The room was full of sludge and sewage. Saskia had lost the books she had borrowed from Oxford, her clothes and her beloved silver bangles. Camille had lost most of her belongings too, but they all managed to get their rucksacks out of the water.

Fran's bag with her money, passport and camera had survived as it had been left on a high shelf attached to the wall. Our Christmas presents were floating around. Her new jacket, the lamp Duncan had bought us from Japan and a few other items were covered in millipedes and frogs. She grabbed whatever she could and quickly left the room.

They all met at the front of the guest house and waited for Thalik's instructions. Decisions had to be made quickly and calm, clear heads were needed. Duncan and Saskia wanted to move away from the sea as soon as possible. Duncan, aware of Saskia's phobia and in an attempt to prepare her for the tough wade ahead through waist-high water, warned her that there could be snakes. Just as Saskia nodded fearfully, they both glanced down to see a long, thin, black snake slivering through the water. Then Thalik pointed to a huge prehistoric looking monitor lizard.

"Do you know why he's here?" he asked. They all shook their heads nervously. "He's come for the flesh."

Rooted to the spot, they watched the lizard as he strolled past, dragging his fat tail behind his massive, six-foot body. His tongue was flapping around as he sampled the air to make sure he was heading in the right direction. The beast swayed from side to side as he walked. Although expert swimmers, the force of the wave had been too much for the hardy Monitor lizards, but this one had somehow survived and emerged from the jungle. Thalik instructed one of his staff to chase the lizard away with a piece of bamboo.

He then told the gathered guests to move to the annexed part of his hotel which was on higher ground. The family, shoeless, set off through the black water. Terrified of more waves they walked in silence, each lost in their thoughts. There were already around twenty shocked tourists there and everybody was trying to make sense of what had happened and remain calm. It was obvious that panic would be counterproductive in such a precarious situation. The hours passed by slowly as they waited for a sign of Luke or me.

Then, in the distance, Fran made out a figure walking through the carnage towards them. It looked like Luke and they all turned towards him, their eyes squinting in the bright sunshine. Nathan was the first to register that it was Luke and started shouting his name and waving, jumping up and down frantically. Luke was hunched over, exhausted, and as he staggered towards them he dropped into a ditch. Everybody gasped but he pulled himself back to his feet and carried on. As he drew nearer, Fran studied his expression. Although he was alone, when he looked up with a wry smile, she knew that I too was alive.

Luke was thrilled that they were all unhurt. They hugged and talked frantically about what had just happened. He told them how his step had quickened in hope when he saw that the devastation was not so bad around this side of the bay. The land was higher. He had prayed his family were alive but all the time he had been filled with panic, imagining life without them, going back to their home in Wandsworth, and how he would he cope. When he first saw his mum his heart filled with joy. He was overwhelmed and couldn't believe that all six of them were alive, waving frantically and shouting at him.

Luke told them that lower down everything was devastated and people were terrified. Time was important and Fran knew that Luke had to return and collect me. She calmed them all down and told Nathan he should accompany Luke back to the village.

Luke and Nathan waved goodbye to the rest of the family not knowing what lay ahead of them or whether they would see one another again. Leaving the security and safety of the family was the hardest thing for Nathan after Luke's warning about the devastation on the other side of the bay.

Thalik told the rest of the family that the monastery on the hill was safe and that the monks would look after them. So they gathered what belongings they had and followed him through the water. They had no shoes so every step was like a game of Russian roulette, but nobody made a fuss. Saskia was terrified of treading on a snake remembering that I had told her that Sri Lanka is home to eighty-three species, five of them poisonous.

They walked on until they found an empty guest house that seemed untouched by the wave. The male owner was rolling up his carpets, otherwise it was deserted. Duncan was dressed in only his boxer shorts, so they asked the owner if he minded them looking for some clothes and he shook his head. The rooms were as the guests had left them and the family felt like they were trespassing.

They found some trousers for Duncan in a deserted room. Fran discovered some cigarettes and a young woman told her to take them. Camille and Fran lit one each. At this point an army officer arrived and shouted at them. Their fears were confirmed. A tsunami had hit Sri Lanka. He told them more waves were on their way. Behind the army officer stood a monk who suggested that they accompany him to the monastery on the hill. It was the safest place to be, out of the reach of the ocean. They followed him, their feet sore and covered in mud.

The road towards the monastery was full of people walking in ripped and tattered clothes, wounded and bleeding. They walked in silence, some badly injured, others in shock. They reached the main road where the monk was waiting with a tuk-tuk ready to give them a lift to the monastery. Presumably this was one of the last vehicles to have petrol and still be in one piece. The driver was revving the engine, desperate to go in case there was another wave. He looked scared and shouted at Pat and his family to hurry up and get in. Camille, Saskia and Fran climbed in next to a man holding his young daughter, but Pat was much slower at walking than the others. The monk was shouting that they had to hurry, so Duncan motioned that he would stay with Pat while the others were to go on ahead.

"Hurry up and find us," called Fran to her husband and son as they screeched off up the side of the hill to safety.

They waved and nodded.

The monastery was at the top of a very steep hill and the tuk-tuks engine spluttered with the weight of all the passengers. When it reached the top they all jumped out and the driver went off to collect more people. They walked into the grounds of the monastery and felt a wave of peace.

It was a hub of activity; the monks making food and drinks for everybody and tending to the injured. People were in shock and crying, standing in all they had left of ripped and torn items of clothing. People were missing, and loved ones sobbed as they waited for news. Fran and her daughters sat on the grass. They sat in silence, digesting the horror, and worrying about the rest of us, praying that we were safe. They had been there for a while, waiting for Pat and Duncan, when the monks started furiously ringing their bell.

They began to shout, "Water coming, water coming!"

Everybody jumped to their feet and ran to look down onto Unawatuna. Fran, Camille and Saskia witnessed the second wave approaching, a wall of water moving across the land taking everything with it. They stood and watched helplessly as the water raced through the village again. The very road they had just come along was now engulfed in water. They were all thinking the same thing. Where were Pat and Duncan? They had left them on that road.

Camille turned to her mum with fear in her eyes.

"Are they all dead?" she asked, as her body went weak.

"Can the waves get up here?" said Saskia, panicking.

"No, of course not," Fran answered both their questions, trying to keep calm so as not to upset her daughters.

They watched in horror as Mother Nature threw herself across the land and spewed the contents of the bay over the village. Somewhere down there was the rest of their family. It didn't matter how high up they were, terror was ingrained. Anything seemed possible; nowhere was safe. Maybe the waves could reach sixty feet; only time would tell.

Fran and Camille were approached by a German man carrying his two-year-old daughter. The little girl was hysterical. He asked if they could look after her as his wife and other child were missing and he needed to go and look for them. He handed Fran his ID card in case something happened to him and he didn't return. They sat and played with the little girl who was terrified and couldn't speak any English. Trying to keep her amused was no easy task, but at least trying to comfort this little girl kept them temporarily occupied. Thankfully, to the joy of all around, he later returned with his wife and other child. The little girl was overwhelmed. The mother ran to her daughter and cried and hugged her. The family of four was at long last reunited.

Fran had some iodine in her medical kit which had survived the water, so she started to help clean people's wounds. She kept one eye on the path waiting for Pat and Duncan. Her fear was growing.

A naked Dutch couple arrived at the monastery. The man had been dragged along by the wave and had smashed into some machinery. He was very badly injured. Fran treated him with iodine which made him yelp. Others gave them clothing. There was a man with a shattered back and a young boy with two broken legs. Nobody could help them – they needed a hospital.

The hours passed and the three of them were having the same thoughts over and over. What had happened to Pat and Duncan? They didn't dare talk about it together so as not to tempt fate. As the hours dragged by, the more worried they became. Eventually, they saw Pat and Duncan limping towards them. Pat explained that they had been told to leave the road and walk up the side of the hill. On the way, they had been invited into a house for hot cups of sweet tea to get their strength up. The detour most probably saved their lives. Pat had wanted to return to Zimmer Rest to see if he could salvage any other belongings and Duncan had had a battle on his hands to prevent him from leaving. A French couple had helped Duncan to dissuade Pat from going back to the village and convinced him to stay and drink tea.

At the monastery, Pat got chatting to an elderly Irish couple from Galway. Although Pat grew up in Sri Lanka his mother had gone back to Ireland to give birth to him. Pat's family is originally from Galway and as coincidence would have it they knew the same people. They had lots to talk about which helped take them away, temporarily, from the horror below them.

The Irish woman described two men she had seen wandering around the streets behind Unawatuna a few hours after the tsunami. Her description could have easily been of Luke and Nathan. This added to Fran and Duncan's fear that something had happened to us. Although they had seen

Luke after the first wave they didn't know what had happened to him and Nathan since then. There were stories aplenty from recent survivors who had made it to the monastery about buildings that had survived the first onslaught only to collapse in the second wave.

Duncan was worried and discussed with Fran the possibility that our guest house may have collapsed but they both tried their hardest to remain positive and not to imagine the worst. Thalik arrived at the monastery for the night and they were happy to see him.

The night drew in and people tried to get some sleep. The air was filled with the sounds of people moaning in pain as they tried to find a comfortable position to lie in. The monk at the monastery stayed awake all night to protect against looters. He was organising food, medicine, water, hot sugary tea for those in shock and distributing oil lamps to keep the mosquitoes away. Everyone was restless, drifting in and out of sleep, jumping at the slightest sound and worrying about what had happened to us in the village.

Duncan had discovered a wallet in the pocket of the trousers he had 'borrowed', so the next morning he set about trying to return it. It was a scary walk but he was adamant that he wanted to take back the wallet as quickly as possible. Once at the guest house he knocked on the door of the room where he had found the trousers. A large, red-faced Englishman opened it. Duncan explained that he had needed to borrow the trousers and apologised profusely. He told the man that he hadn't seen the wallet until he was at the monastery and was sorry for any inconvenience. Thinking the bloke would be overjoyed, he was shocked when he abruptly told him that the trousers were his son's favourite pair and asked him to remove them. Duncan took them off and was left standing in his underwear.

As he was about to shut the door, Duncan asked if him if he had any other trousers he could give him, repeating that he had lost all of his clothes in the tsunami. Reluctantly the bloke gave him a pair of extra large trousers. Duncan had no choice but to take them to cover his modesty. He walked away in his new mustard-coloured trousers, miserably clutching the waistband in his dirty hands, and headed back to the monastery.

Fran was desperate to know that we were unharmed in the village and Duncan offered to walk down and find us. Thalik said he would accompany Duncan as he knew the way, but that they had to be quick as it had been reported on the radio that another wave was on its way.

"I think she not be lucky. I saw your brothers but not Tracey," he said, shaking his head. Thalik was sure that I was dead.

Duncan mentally processed this comment together with the description that the Irish woman had given him of what may have been Luke and Nathan running. He was starting to think something terrible had happened. They set off down the hill towards the village and away from the safety of the monastery.

The smell of death was in the air. Duncan didn't know what he was going to have to face and fear was starting to grip him. Thalik refused to walk on the beach and insisted on taking the back roads which were utterly devastated. The walk was terrifying, listening to the sea, as they weaved through smashed houses and past dead people. Every footstep took them further away from the monastery and closer to the village.

Thalik put himself in this dangerous situation, despite being terrified himself. He remained, like a loyal friend, by Duncan's side. There was no hidden agenda, just human kindness. They arrived at a house which was full of dead bodies. Thalik told poor Duncan to look for me inside. His legs were shaking and his mouth went dry as he entered the house. A rancid smell took his breath away, but he was sure no western bodies were in there. They continued towards The Village Inn. They walked in silence mostly, too shocked by the images surrounding them to talk, until they found the remains of the guest house. Only two buildings were still standing, everything next to them had collapsed.

It all looked very different now and it was hard to get their bearings. Duncan felt sick. There was a Sri Lankan man standing by the entrance to the flattened building, obviously in shock. Duncan begged Thalik to ask if any westerners had died at the Village Inn. Frightened, he watched Thalik and the other man talk. Everything happened in slow motion and it seemed to take an eternity for the man to answer. Thalik turned to Duncan and shook his head. Duncan punched the air with relief as his vision blurred with tears. The man told Thalik that the tourists that had survived had ended up congregating at The Rock, a short walk away. They turned and headed in that direction. Upon arriving there, they immediately saw Luke and Nathan milling around, but no sign of me. Unaware that they thought I was dead, I shouted down to Duncan and Thalik from the balcony and waved. I raced down the stairs to see them.

"Fuck, am I glad to see you," Duncan said as we hugged.

"Charming!" I laughed.

Then we all noticed Duncan's trousers and our laughter rang out. He was pale and shaking. I had no idea what they had just gone through or their fears that I was dead. Thalik embraced me and slapped my back repeatedly. For a small man he had a strong arm, as he slapped the air out of my lungs and grinned.

"I thought you no more," he said.

Duncan explained that they had found shelter at a monastery and that the family wanted us to leave with him. We discussed our options. I didn't fancy leaving the safety of The Rock and walking for at least forty or fifty minutes. Duncan and Thalik understood this as they themselves had just done it. After talking to Luke, we decided to stay as we felt safe and wanted to be of some help. I felt bad that they had come all this way for us but we had made our decision. There was no time to waste and Duncan and Thalik set off back to the monastery and the family alone.

"Be careful and hurry up you two," I said, and stuck up my thumbs.

Duncan and Thalik raced back to the monastery to share the news that they had found us all alive at The Rock. Everyone was overjoyed. Thalik had suggested that they move to a hotel with a pool just below the monastery on the other side of the hill. So they gathered their belongings and thanked the monks for their kindness. Fran and the family walked down the hill to the hotel and were delighted to find that the pool was still functioning so they could take a swim and dry out their belongings. They hung their damp clothes over the rocks, but there was nowhere to wash them.

They all sat on the grass and felt better, knowing that the three of us were alive. But Fran had heard a rumour that the High Commission was putting buses on from this hotel and was determined to go to The Rock herself to bring us back. Pat felt this was interfering as we had said that we wanted to stay down there and help as much as we could. But Fran was adamant. She was coming to get us. They started to prepare themselves.

17 – THE WOMAN ON THE BENCH

Dammika arrived with his surviving relatives from The Village Inn and told me that they were going to go and get his father's body. It was trapped underneath the house. I decided to accompany them, ready to help if need be.

When we got there, they started to move all the debris from the collapsed house to the side. The mud was really deep and it was hard for them to keep their balance. They talked loudly in Sinhalese and, although I didn't understand, I could tell by their tone that they were talking about the old man. Their voices were sad and hollow. They climbed over the smashed concrete walls and I knew they had found him when I heard their panicked voices and the sound of crying.

They pulled his frail body out of the collapsed house and their cheeks were wet with tears. He looked as though he was asleep except that his skin was a bluish white tone. They placed him on a board and collected plastic bowls full of sea water. They caressed his body as they gently washed the mud off him. His body was stiff and his skin was taut around his rib cage. He was still wearing his white vest, now dirty and torn. They tied his big toes together with string and pulled at his fingers so that they could fold his hands together. They then wrapped him in a sheet and kissed him. They were incredibly composed but I could tell they were devastated.

Every evening on our way out to the bar we had say hello to this old man, sitting on his verandah amongst the tropical flowers, dressed in his vest. Now I was witnessing him being taken to his grave. I left them to take their father to rest and went to find Luke. I felt very strange as if I had known him well, but I had merely said hello to him on several occasions. I still felt a connection.

I was snapped back to reality.

"You've done bodies before haven't you?" Jamie was standing there.

"Yes," I said, hesitantly.

The body of a western woman had been found and the Sri Lankan men were too respectful to wrap her body – they wanted another western woman to prepare her for burial. She was in her swimming costume. Jamie said he would come with me. I was grateful and went to gather some sheets. Jamie and I left with another bloke, Mike, for our grisly walk to find the woman. We didn't know one another at all but here we were in the most surreal situation together. I could feel our mutual tension and anxiety as we walked. We made conversation about our lives at home and even managed to share a joke.

Mike was a real pain. He had been quite a scaremonger on The Rock. I had put it down to shock but didn't like him much. He kept going on and on about the next wave causing people to panic. Luke had told me not to listen so I had ignored him most of the time.

The woman's body was quite a walk away and I started to get a clearer picture of how far the wave had reached. It looked as though it had been at its maximum force at the village. Then it had swept some way up the hill before returning down to where Luke's family had been staying. It had spat bodies out onto the road, turned on itself and left. The hill seemed to have broken some of the wave's momentum.

This really was like a scene from a war film with bodies lying in pools of blood. I couldn't really comprehend that they were corpses. Someone had placed banana leaves over their faces to give them some dignity, but it was still horrible. We walked in silence past the stiff bodies. Some of the victims' arms were raised up as if trying to save themselves. I kept telling myself not to look but my eyes kept glancing from side to side, filling my brain with horrible images.

Then we spotted a western man with a huge camera taking photos of the dead people's faces. He was removing the banana leaves and snapping away. We were horrified and stopped to ask him what he was doing. I had presumed he was a journalist but he told us that he was taking photographs for identification purposes.

Up ahead I could see a body, her face and body partially covered by a towel, lying on a bench. My mouth went dry and my heart was racing. It must be her, I thought. I could see that the feet sticking out from under the towel were white. I felt sick. The sun was beating down, but the ground was still really slippery.

As we approached her, we realised that she must have been lifted off the ground onto the bench. We stood there for what seemed like an eternity, knowing that we had to remove the towel but none of us wanting to. Finally, Jamie pulled it back to reveal her face. I felt the air leave my body. A swarm of flies flew at us and I screamed. I felt revolted but knew it was terrible to feel like this. Her face was swollen and blue, her eyes were closed and her top lip was slightly upturned, exposing white teeth. She had short, curly, blonde hair, was wearing jewellery and had painted nails. I felt tremendous sorrow. She was quite a thickset woman and I was disgusted when Mike referred to her as a beached whale. I told him to shut up and piss off. She was a normal, middle-aged woman. She was in her mid-fifties, about the same age as my mum.

She was too heavy for us to lift her body and so we placed the sheet we had brought with us onto the ground and tried to angle the bench forwards. The time it took for her body to roll off the bench and hit the ground seemed to go in slow motion. Her body landed with a dull thud. I cringed, my toes curled up, and I looked away. I wanted to vomit as her now stiff body wobbled with the impact of hitting the hard ground. Her head was bleeding and I hoped we hadn't caused this.

"I'm so sorry my darling," I found myself saying over and over again.

It was undignified but there was no easy way around this. We wrapped her up and managed to lift her back onto the bench. I was shocked by how many flies were swarming around her. I remember thinking, somewhere people love this lady and she means the world to them. She will surely be missed. People's lives will be ruined. What if this was my mum, I knew how it would rip our family apart. This poor woman was on her holiday and now she was dead, surrounded by three strangers.

Boxing Day would never be the same for her family. Christmas would, from now on, be a time of great upset. Here were strangers wrapping up a dead woman, with no way of knowing who she was. We couldn't even let her family know to save them some anguish. Somewhere, somebody would be putting her on a missing list. A family would be distraught, waiting, maybe trying to book a flight out to Sri Lanka to find her. They would be worried that that they hadn't heard from their mum since the tsunami. They would be sitting by their phone and jumping every time it rang. What if her husband was here and had survived? He needed to know where she was. Maybe he was another victim. There were no other western bodies on this hill. I could tell that she hadn't been living in Sri Lanka or was married to a local man because the suntan marks on her back were relatively new.

We left her wrapped up in the sheet, lying alone on the bench. We had done our job. My selfish side was relieved that I was going back to Luke, but I also felt guilty leaving her there alone, in a strange country. I shook these thoughts out of my head as I turned away. The thing I was finding hardest to come to terms with was how one second people had been talking, laughing, and eating their breakfast, and the next moment they were dead. How quickly a life can be taken. It was so easy to die once your lungs had stopped working.

We started to walk back in silence, lost in our own thoughts. I regret more than anything that we didn't say a prayer for her but, at the time, it didn't enter my head. All I could see was her face. She looked so kind and had crow's feet around her eyes, so she obviously liked a laugh. I imagined her excitedly packing her suitcase for her Christmas break and calling family and friends before she got her flight to wish them all a happy Christmas. Not once would she have thought that this would be the last time she ever shut the front door behind her. Tears rolled down my face.

A Sri Lankan man ran towards us and gave us the passport of a western woman that he had found. I looked at the sodden photograph and recognised her from The Rock. At least she was alive. Another man walked by me in tears. He was swinging his arms, as if he was marching. I stopped to talk with him. His clothes were in tatters and at first I couldn't understand what he was saying as he was sobbing so much. His English was good so I had no problem understanding him once his sobs had subsided. He told me his whole family was missing. His hands were trembling and his teeth were chattering as if he was freezing cold. He had the same fear in his eyes as that of baby Harry's brother and sister and his big, sad eyes bore into my soul. He asked if I could go to his house with him. He had a kind face and neatly cut short, silver hair. The swinging of his arms was obviously an attempt to comfort himself. I hugged his slender frame. He felt so fragile, as though he could snap.

"Please help me, I'm very worried, please can you help miss?" he kept begging me.

I knew deep down that I would be of no use to him but went with him to his house anyway. We couldn't get in because all the broken furniture was piled up at the door. We pushed and pulled but it wouldn't budge. The mud outside his house was over my ankles and created an amazingly strong suction. I was hardly able to pull my feet free let alone move this debris. We started trying to dig up the thick mud with wooden planks but it was pointless. As much as we tried to pile it up it all slid back. I was terrified of what might be behind the door but knew that there could not be anyone alive as there were no cries for help. I explained to the man that we couldn't do this alone and that we needed help. He was panic stricken and crying desperately. I held his hand and told him to come with me to get help. We walked, holding hands, through the debris. His grief was noticed by all around and people looked with pity at this poor soul.

We returned to The Rock and I explained to Luke and Nathan what had happened to the man. They followed us back and together we tried to move the furniture and other debris but it was obvious we needed machinery to move the obstruction. We brought the man back with us and gave him some water. A local woman came over to talk to him. I saw her embrace him and he sobbed into her chest. His grief was enormous and I couldn't conceive how he would start to rebuild his life. If it was me and all my family and loved ones were gone, I don't think I would want to go on. I said a silent prayer for him.

One of the few happy endings I witnessed was when the young woman with the internal injuries and vine-shaped triffid wound recognised her husband as he arrived at The Rock. Her shriek of delight was the only time we felt overwhelmed with happiness. She couldn't stand up, so he dropped to the ground and embraced her with all his might. They cried and laughed and hugged. I watched her stroke his bruised face with disbelief as though she thought she was dreaming. We all spontaneously clapped with joy.

18 – THE HELICOPTER

A helicopter flew overhead, its propeller thumping in the air. People started shouting and waving and we watched as it flew off into the distance.

"The Indian Army," a small Sri Lankan man told me.

An elderly Sri Lankan man climbed onto the roof of a house. He was holding something under his arm. When he had steadied himself he shook out a red blanket. He was trying to draw attention to our group of survivors.

The helicopter flew around in circles and then left. We watched it get smaller as it headed over the jungle. I wondered if the old man with his blanket was aware of the food and water shortage. We had all just taken what we were given.

Later the air was filled again with the sounds of a helicopter. The sound was similar to that of the tsunami and I felt the adrenalin start to race through my veins. Somewhere, locked in my head, was a trauma associated with this noise. My friend at the zoo, Mandy, had suffered this after hearing the roar of the elephant as Jim was attacked. Many months after the incident she had been at a garden centre in Devon when a low flying jet had roared over.

The noise had frightened her so much she dropped to her knees in fear and cried uncontrollably.

There was lots of speculation about the helicopter. An Indian Diplomat and his family had been holidaying in Unawatuna, and some believed that the helicopter had come to collect him and his family. Others suggested that they were surveying the area with film crews to get a clearer picture of the destruction. We sat and waited.

The good news came that the British High Commission knew we were here. An army soldier had found The Rock. It was a relief to see him walking towards us. We all surrounded him and he told us that they would be able to get the injured and bereaved out to Colombo. The crowd stood and listened. We all had one question on our minds – were more waves forecast? He reassured us that no more waves were expected.

"It's over," he said confidently, "The disaster is finished."

He told us that the epicentre of the 9.0 magnitude quake was under the Indian Ocean near the west coast of Indonesia. This still held no relevance to me so I was confused as I listened to him. Why would an earthquake in Sumatra affect us? Sri Lanka was about 1,000 miles west from the epicentre. He explained that the earthquake had caused huge tsunamis around Asia. It was the biggest earthquake for forty years and possibly the biggest recorded in history. Hundreds of thousands of people had died.

"We were lucky," he said. "It's finished," he told us again, in his heavy Indian accent.

Relief washed over me. I felt happy but weak. Everybody started to digest this information and chat amongst themselves. I just wanted to get home now. The survival instinct is a very strange thing, you really do think primarily of yourself. I felt the sort of relief you experience at the end of a rollercoaster ride: giddy, exhausted, shaky and thankful it was over.

A helicopter had landed on the beach in order to start taking people to Colombo Hospital. It was decided that Stuart would be one of the first. It was a miracle that this old chap had lasted so long. He had the strength of an ox. Luke and Nathan helped carry him in his chair down to the beach. I waved goodbye as they all struggled through the sand and hoped he would make it. I was sure he would as he was a real fighter. The injured and bereaved were all sitting in silence in chairs waiting to see who would go first. There was no arguing.

The area for the injured was right next to the makeshift morgue which must have been awful for them. Many couldn't walk so they were stuck there. The helicopter could only carry six at a time so it was those with the worst injuries who would go first and then the bereaved. After that it would be families with young children, women, and then men. We all agreed that this was right. Obviously everybody wanted to leave but they were gracious. Having been reassured that there were no more waves on the way had reassured us we could be more patient. The westerners who had been staying at The Rock when the wave came hadn't been as traumatised as the rest of us. They had woken up after it all happened and were much calmer. We were grateful for their help and organisation. Like lines of ants, the men carried the injured to the beach.

The Dutch couple, whose daughter had died, decided the mass grave was too frightening and that they couldn't bury the little soul there. I completely understood this. They had been looking for somewhere else to bury their child but still couldn't bear the thought of leaving her here. Then we learned that somebody had organised for the body to be flown out to the city. The dad, still cradling the body of his child in the red towel, had a seat on the helicopter bound for Colombo hospital. His wife just sat staring into space with tears rolling down her face. She and their other two children would follow after. I watched the father, helped by Linda's husband Dave, on his sad walk to the helicopter waiting on the beach.

Then, as I stared into the distance, I was overjoyed to see Pat, Fran, Camille, Duncan, still in his ridiculous trousers, Saskia and Thalik walking towards us. We all hugged. It was a miracle we were all alive. Nathan cried he was so happy. We were all talking at once trying to exchange our stories and none of us were making any sense. It was difficult to show too much excitement as we were aware that so many people around us had not been as lucky.

19 – THE HOTEL ON THE HILL

It was time to leave The Rock. We felt guilty and had mixed feelings. Pat told us we had done as much as we could to help. The Sri Lankan people needed the army now. He was right, but this had been our home. I felt close to everybody here despite only having known them for a couple of days. Even as we protested, Pat and Fran would have none of it. They were in charge and had sensibly decided that it was time to go. They had to think about getting all eight of us out safely.

I went to find Linda, the woman who had sent our text on the night of the tsunami. I said goodbye and wished her and her family a safe journey. She had been a great support to me that night and I was very grateful. I also said goodbye to the lads we had spent time with and wished them a safe trip home. Andy looked terrible. I told him to be strong.

We collected what things we had. As we walked down the dusty path carved out by the kids on the digger, I looked for Dammika but he was nowhere to be seen. We left with a mixture of sadness and relief. I turned to take one more look at The Rock. The Sri Lankan women were still cooking in their huge pots. The injured were waiting for helicopters to take them to Colombo. The flies buzzed around their wounds but not one of them moaned. It looked like a stage set; nothing seemed real anymore. I blew a kiss and turned to follow the rest of the family. I felt like I was saying goodbye to a friend.

We now had to get to the hill on the other side of the village. Back down into the war zone. I was nervous and not entirely convinced that there wouldn't be another wave. We looked back one last time and waved goodbye to our friends. We had enjoyed the same walk through the village every night before the tsunami. Happy, warm evenings, tropical beach bars, spoilt for choice. Every single one of the bars that lined the beach was ruined. The road was empty, save for an occasional person walking by.

I got out my camera and took some photos of the carnage. I would not need reminding of these images, but wanted to have something to show family and friends and maybe my children and grandchildren in the future. The sun was beating down on us. It was quicker to walk on the beach but I couldn't bring myself to go there as I knew there would be bodies washed up on the shore and I had seen enough. So the group split. Fran and Camille walked with me on what was left of the road. It seemed to take an eternity. Looking around, everywhere was the same, and there was an eerie silence. My legs felt as though they had lead weights tied to them. I was finding it hard to walk. I was dazed, as if I was on Valium, and nothing seemed to make sense.

We walked on, the sweat was running down my back, but I could see the hill now and knew we were getting closer. Small dogs lay curled up on the side of the roads. They were obviously dying but there was nothing we could do. We had no clean water to give them. We passed folded houses, broken concrete walls and upside down cars. People were wandering through the debris, searching, without even the energy to look up at us as we passed.

Most of the shops had been smashed up and what was left of them had clearly been looted. We saw safes lying on the ground with their doors sawn off. Who could blame them, I thought. So many people had been left with nothing, only the clothes they stood up in. Maybe the looters had had nothing their whole lives and the tsunami had given them a chance to start afresh. Normally I would be aghast, but this seemed different.

I started wondering if people at home knew what was happening and thought about all the times I had seen footage of floods in Bangladesh on the television with the odd roof popping above water level and somebody holding on for dear life. I would watch in horror and then the next news story would come on and I would immediately forget about that person. I promised myself that I would never be like that again.

We started to walk up the hill. Every step meant we were getting away from the sea which was comforting, but still I was scared. Not even the thought of being higher up could make me feel happy; too much had happened. I cried for the people we had left behind and prayed they would be safe. This place was much higher than The Rock, but I still felt vulnerable, nowhere seemed high enough. My imagination played havoc with me and images of huge waves kept pushing to the front of my mind. No matter how hard I tried to suppress these feelings they kept coming. I thought it strange that my brain was not protecting me against these irrational fears and helping me cope with the situation but it did just the opposite.

It felt surreal as we walked into the gardens of the hotel. It was calm with hammocks swinging gently by the swimming pool. I could almost forget about the dreadful scenes at the foot of the hill but my mind wouldn't let me. Fran had hung up their salvaged clothes and rucksacks to dry, the smell of sewage made me wretch but there was nowhere to wash them. Clean water was precious. I know we looked absolutely awful and I felt embarrassed by my appearance. Down in the village everybody looked the same and didn't bat an eyelid, but here people were well groomed and no doubt horrified at the sight of us. I dipped my feet into the pool's cool water and wriggled my toes around. The muck on them slowly started to disintegrate. My chipped toenail paint was the only damage to my feet. A dip in the pool to try and freshen up was what we done. I looked out at the sea and thought about our weakness and stupidity as humans. We think that we run this planet. We can build the highest buildings, invent nuclear bombs, fly to the moon but really that is nothing compared to what Mother Nature can do. We had experienced first-hand the force that really runs this planet and she had given us a reminder here in Asia of what she is capable of inflicting on us.

I could see the village in the distance and could just make out The Rock. I felt very guilty that we had deserted everyone there. We hadn't even paid Dammika for the five nights we had stayed at his place. We could have left the money we owed with somebody, but we just didn't think. He would be in desperate need of money now that he had lost everything. I knew that I couldn't bring this to Luke's attention now because he would march straight off to find him. Luke was safe on the hill and this is where I wanted him. I decided that I would sort out Dammika's money when we got home. I swung in a hammock and cried until no more tears would come. I think this crying was a mixture of relief and grief. I could cry properly now and let my guard down. It had seemed wrong to cry when we were with the Sri Lankan people. They were the ones who needed to grieve, not us.

We sat on the grass by the pool exchanging horror stories from the past two days. Everybody looked different, I thought, and they had a haunted look about their faces. We kept going over and over our experiences hoping to make sense of this disaster. All the time I kept looking out to the ocean, knowing I would never feel the same about it now that it was tainted.

Poor Pat had some very nasty cuts on his toes and had burnt the soles of his feet when he had given his shoes away to somebody in need of them. Walking on the scorching hot ground had caused the soles of his feet to blister. The flies had taken a shine to Pat's feet so we poured iodine on them. Pat winced, his knuckles were white.

Fran, Camille, Duncan and Saskia also had wounds on their feet. Some were deep gashes so we cleaned and bandaged them with what we had. I tended to Duncan's feet and we laughed as he reminded us of a Tom and Jerry cartoon with his huge, exaggerated bandages.

Young Sri Lankan men were handing out packages of rice and dahl, wrapped in newspaper, and still warm, from a vehicle. Again I was amazed at their kindness and efficiency. Who was cooking all this food? We accepted the packages gratefully and the food inside was lovely and fresh. We devoured the food like the thirsty dogs had devoured their water the night before.

Pat remembered that he had some wine in his rucksack, so we cracked it open and cut empty plastic bottles in half to make wine glasses. Fran had managed to acquire two packets of cigarettes.

"Cheers!" we all said, as we knocked our plastic cups together.

We sat and chatted for hours until everybody felt tired. We decided it was time to try and get some sleep and so brushed our teeth with toothpaste, but no water, which made me gag, and said our goodnights.

Just before we retired for the night, Fran exclaimed, "Oh no!" We all turned around in fear. "Our things have been stolen!" she cried.

Someone had rifled through their bags and had also been through the clothes left hanging up to dry. Two digital cameras, Camille's mobile phone and some money were missing. All of their travellers-cheques had also been taken. These had been cut along the stubs leaving their serial numbers, presumably so that we could claim them back on insurance. This looked like the work of westerners. It was too well thought out. A Sri Lankan would have no reason to take travellers-cheques and, if they had, they certainly wouldn't have cut the cheques in this way, nor would they have taken a tube of moisturiser. After everything we had all been through this was the final straw. But we needed to sleep and decided to deal with it in the morning.

The stars and moon lit the grass where we were lying out in the open. Even up here, I caught myself listening to the ocean, just in case. Pat, Luke and I settled down to sleep using our rucksacks as pillows and holding on tightly to our meagre possessions, aware that there was a thief in the camp. The others slept in a makeshift dorm. I watched fruit bats flying over us, listened to the frogs croaking, and Pat beside me snoring. As I drifted off to sleep, the usual thoughts of my family and friends ran through my mind. I wanted so much to be able to talk to them. Throughout the night I would wake with a start, sit bolt upright, sweating, in a panic. This was to become the norm for me over the next few days; nightmares about waves, dead people, confusion and horror.

Pat was snoring so loudly that dark figures trying to sleep in the hammocks began shouting at him to shut up. One threw a plastic bottle in our direction but luckily it missed us. Pat was oblivious. I smiled to myself, grateful to hear him snore. He was alive.

The next morning, the talk was of buses arriving from Colombo. I was stiff from sleeping on the ground and my clothes were grass stained. My arms and legs were covered in mosquito bites and I felt really grubby. I scooped some water from the swimming pool and went behind a rock to wash. Thalik arrived at the hotel and waited with us for the buses to arrive. Exhaustion had set in. I felt weak and emotional. Walking around, not knowing what to do, agitated and restless, I started looking at people and hating them for all the trivial things they were whinging about. People were running about, complaining that there weren't enough bread rolls for those tourists who had paid to stay at the hotel. They made me sick. I realised I had to calm down. I knew that my anger was part of my post-traumatic stress, but I could have physically throttled them. I sat on a hammock and looked down towards the village. We were leaving, going home back to our lovely home and kittens in London. I felt tremendous guilt for the people we were leaving behind, but also a desperate need to feel safe and happy in the company of family and friends.

The tears started again, stinging my eyes. I tasted their salt on my lips and tried to stifle my sobs, but with no luck. I could still make no sense of what had happened. I just lay there supine whilst people were organising names for the bus. I had run out of steam and was no use to anybody. A woman approached me. She looked calm and had a kind face. She told me her name was Sarah and that she was a homeopath from England. She offered to give me something to help with the trauma I was experiencing. I readily agreed to try some of her tablets. I felt embarrassed by my appearance as her clothes were immaculate. She had actually been staying at this hotel when the tsunami hit, and that's why she looked so good. She also offered some tablets to Nathan, instructing us to put these small white crystals under our tongues and to let them dissolve. She explained that we would feel very emotional but that it was healthy for us to release these feelings. She filled a small bag with these tiny crystals and told us to take three a day for the next two days. The wave of emotion I experienced from taking these tablets was immediate and the tears began again.

20 – THE BUS JOURNEY

It was mid-morning already and the sun was beating down. We all looked like we had chicken pox with our huge mosquito bites. I hope we don't get Malaria, I thought.

Thalik walked across the garden with a small rucksack on his back. Smiling, he told us that the buses had arrived and were on the road, ready to start evacuating the tourists. We had to leave. Walk away from all these poor people. Nobody would come to help them. They had no safe bolt-hole like us.

I sensed a feeling of ill-will towards us from some of the other tourists. I suspected that this was because we hadn't been staying at the hotel and so shouldn't expect to be first in the queue to get on the buses. They kept talking about the numbers being more than those originally staying at the hotel. Admittedly, we were a large group, but we weren't getting separated again. Either, we all got on a bus together or none of us got on. A meeting was called and Fran hastened over. I watched from the hammock, enraged. One idiot was filming the meeting and others were smiling and waving at him, laughing about the tsunami. They were so far removed from it all. I willed him to turn around and point his camera in my direction. I would give him two fingers. I felt as though I was possessed. I needed to chill out, so I diverted my gaze away from everything that was making my blood boil and looked instead at some passion flowers creeping over a wall with their plump, orange fruits dangling.

Eventually we were told that we could all have seats on one of the buses. I remained lying in the hammock. It was so different from The Rock. There, people were injured and bereaved, but everybody was gracious about helping each other. Maybe it was because we looked like down and outs, our hair greasy and our clothes grubby. Maybe if we looked like we normally did in London we might have been thought of differently. Maybe if they knew how we had tried to help people in the village, and the horrible things we had seen, they might have thought twice and understood why we looked as we did.

We collected our belongings and Thalik led us down the hill to the waiting vehicles. He was so lovely and upbeat, despite the fact that his business and belongings were destroyed. I suppose his Buddhist faith was his crutch. Again, there were horrors all around us. People were scrambling around in the debris. One family was removing metal corrugated sheets off their tuk-tuk. It was flattened, their source of income ruined, and they looked devastated. Huge sheets of jagged glass stood up like mini glaciers. The scale of the damage was vast.

As we approached our buses, the Sri Lankan people looked up from what they were doing, smiled and waved goodbye. I raised my hand in a half wave and tried to smile at their kind faces. I felt terrible as if we were royalty being collected. I tried not to look at the sea, too scared in case it started rushing towards us. My chest tightened and I felt tears pricking at my eyes. I knew I had to say goodbye to our friend Thalik and leave him here. Thalik laughed and put his arms around me and patted my back again.

"Why are you crying?" he said. "You can go now!"

I smiled at him. It was true I could go, and there wasn't any point trying to explain to him what I was feeling as he was evidently delighted that we were able to leave. We all kissed him goodbye. He had been such a kind, generous person throughout this whole terrible tragedy. I will never forget him. His unselfishness was a lesson to us all. He promised Saskia that he would try to find her jewellery and said he hoped to meet up with us in the north, where we were headed. He was going to start cleaning up Zimmer Rest and then go to Kandy to stay with relatives for a while.

We all thanked him from the bottom of our hearts, knowing we had made a friend for life. We got onto the bus and found our seats. The driver turned on the ignition and pulled away. Thalik waited outside with everyone else who had gathered on the road to wave us off. He smiled enthusiastically as I blew him a kiss. I felt a huge sadness as I sank into my seat and watched their smiling faces disappear in the distance. Luke put his arms around me and I cried into his chest.

Temporary roads had been cleared. I wondered if the bus drivers had been paid extra to travel down south. As we left for Galle, I noticed the Buddha statue was standing, unscathed and still shiny gold, overlooking the bay. I hoped he would look after the people of Unawatuna. Just before we passed the monastery, Camille asked the driver to stop in case there were any other tourists left there. We all watched in amazement as she ran like a gazelle up the steps of the hill to the top. She returned with nobody in tow. They had all left already. People clapped as she got back onto the bus, much to Camille's horror. We laughed at how fast she had run up those steep steps.

In Galle there were huge fishing boats on their sides, everywhere was flattened and people were standing around looking dazed. I fidgeted in my seat as the bus drove next to the ocean. There were piles upon piles of debris and I couldn't make out what anything was, except for the boats. Previously, Galle had been a vibrant, busy town. I remembered us climbing off the train and how the touts had hassled us. The frenzy had been replaced by this empty shell, like a war zone. Apart from the obvious death toll, thousands more had lost their homes and had their livelihoods destroyed. It was hard to take in.

The train station we had emerged from a few days before was a wreck. Out at sea, we could see a war ship on its side. They must all have died on there. The chaos was unimaginable. How would they start to rebuild this place? All the time, there was this nagging thought at the back of my mind, reminding me that we were not safe yet. There was another eight hours to Colombo. A man reached out his hand to me and mimed that he needed a drink but I had no water. The railway track looked as though a giant had walked along it, ripping it up as if it was a toy and tossing pieces into the jungle. Every now and again a concrete skeleton of a house could be seen standing empty, ghostly, a lone curtain blowing in the breeze. Where were the families that had occupied these trashed buildings? Shoes, cars, tuk-tuks, fabrics, slabs of broken concrete, and wrecked boats.

To my horror heavy rain began pelting the bus. As if these people hadn't had enough to deal with, I watched through the window as the makeshift roads turned to mud. The day after Jim had died at the zoo it had rained and I had wondered whether it was him crying for what had happened. Was this downpour the deceased Sri Lankan and western people crying for what had happened here? The roads were turning into little streams.

One summer, Luke and I had been caught in a flood in Le Puy in France. While camping, a huge thunder storm had unleashed hail stones as big as golf balls. They pitted our car, creating dents all over the bodywork. Then came relentless rain and everything started getting washed away peoples tents, tables, chairs and gazebos. I was scared.

We were all quiet on the bus; lost in our own fears. Two kids to my left were reading books. Thankfully they weren't looking out of the windows. This was bad enough for the adults let alone their innocent eyes. I tried to read, but couldn't. I tried to sleep, but couldn't. I was worried that we would be caught up in a flood.

We passed more railway tracks, the metal twisted and bent. I recalled our journey on the Queen of the Sea and how crowded it had been the week before. The passengers wouldn't have stood a chance. The metal bars on the windows would have prevented people from escaping.

I was later to learn that an estimated seventeen hundred people lost their lives on that train. The wave hurled the carriages into the jungle like cardboard boxes. The destruction of the Queen of the Sea was to become the world's worst rail disaster in history. For a country so small the death toll from the train alone was gigantic. Only around one hundred and fifty passengers managed to escape from the train, the rest perished.

Halfway to Colombo we stopped for a toilet break. There was a small shop where we could get refreshments and we bought some chocolate, Bombay Mix, water and crackers – a strange combination but there wasn't much choice. We re-boarded the bus and started the second leg of our journey. The Bombay mix was really hot, the crackers were dry and the chocolate quickly melted but it felt like a feast. Camille and Nathan engaged in a cracker eating contest and we laughed as the crumbs started to fly. It was good to see the kids to our left also chuckling away. It was the first time we had all laughed properly for ages. Then we noticed that the rain outside had stopped.

The same picture unfolded along every metre of the coastline. The palm trees stood proud all the way back to Colombo, only the occasional one on its side. I guessed that they had either been hit by a large fishing boat or were probably diseased already and not strong enough to withstand the wave. I had become used to the carnage outside the window. Upturned fishing boats in the trees and vast empty spaces. We sat for hours on that coach. Rumours in the south had suggested that the airport had been washed away including planes on the runway and that Colombo was destroyed.

Thankfully the suburbs of Colombo appeared untouched and looked normal. Women were walking around in multi-coloured clothes, carrying parasols to protect them from the hot rays of the sun. The street vendors were still selling their wares. There was the same busy traffic and endless tooting of car horns. Nothing had changed. They must have wondered why the tourists on the buses all had the same, haunted white faces, some dressed in rags with dirty bandages and bruises. For those people in Colombo, the tsunami was a million miles away.

21 – COLOMBO, AGAIN

When we arrived in Colombo it looked the same as the morning that we had left, heading south for Christmas. The bus pulled into the driveway of a conference centre set up as a refugee camp for all of the survivors. We were greeted by the press, filming people as they got off the bus, trying to get snippets of information from survivors, working their way around the injured. We went inside to find that they had set up a restaurant, a doctor's surgery and an optician who would test your eyes and give you new glasses within three hours. There was internet access, mobile phones and television screens showed images of devastated Asia. New clothes had been donated by local shops and it was like a huge jumble sale. There were showers with hot running water and soap. The main conference room had been turned into a huge dormitory with a few hundred beds, all dressed in crisp white sheets with folded towels on them. Unfortunately, this reminded me of the makeshift morgue at The Rock. I pulled Pat aside and told him that I didn't want to stay here because it made me anxious and, to my relief, everybody felt the same. Pat decided that we needed to see if we could find somewhere more relaxing.

We ate the delicious food they had prepared and chatted to some of the other survivors. Everybody there had a story. We then washed and were about to leave when we bumped into Christine and her husband, a middle-aged couple from London. The last time I had seen them was Christmas night as were leaving the beach to go to bed early. They had been staying in a hut nearby and we had seen them every day on the beach. The last thing Christine's husband had said to me that night was, "aren't we lucky," as he held up his glass of Bailey's Irish Cream to toast us.

They told us that on the morning of the tsunami they decided to take a boat trip which had saved their lives. The tsunami had travelled underneath the boat without them even realizing it. Christine told us how all of a sudden the ocean was full of the most beautiful tropical fish flapping around on the surface, all the colours of the rainbow. They had been delighted by their sudden appearance, but the Sri Lankan boatman had started to panic and told them something was wrong. At first, they thought he was over reacting but he was adamant that they had to return to land.

As they started to make their way back to shore, they saw televisions bobbing around in the water and the couple's first reaction was disgust at the thought of people throwing their old appliances into the sea. When they saw fridges and tables, they began to realise something was seriously wrong. Then they saw bodies floating face down amongst the other flotsam. Approaching the beach they understood something terrible had happened. Everything had gone. They were scared and didn't know what to do. Their beach hut had been washed away. Had they been there that morning they would most probably have died. All the usual landmarks had vanished; the bars and restaurants were destroyed. Only the concrete shells remained. Now, they were now trying to book a flight home and so we said our goodbyes. I never saw them again.

The first thing I wanted to do was to find a telephone in order to ring home. I dialled my mum's number; it rang only once before she answered.

"Mum, it's me!" I yelled. "We're alive, we're ok, safe in Colombo, don't worry!"

The relief in my mum's voice was overwhelming. I had to be quick as people were waiting to use the phone and we still had to find somewhere to stay. Night time was creeping up on us. After a brief conversation I said my goodbyes and hung up. Camille and Saskia also made quick phone calls before we left the conference centre and hailed two tuk-tuks. Their prices had shot up since the disaster. It seemed like a fast track to make extra cash on the back of what had happened.

The four of us returned to Shrubbery Gardens where we had stayed on our arrival in Sri Lanka. It felt good to be back in familiar surroundings. The pretty road leading to the guest house had masses of magenta bougainvillea cascading over the walls. Mrs. Settupathy recognised us straight away and welcomed us in. Luckily she had two double rooms on the ground floor free. I wasn't that comfortable with the ground floor but we took them anyway. She told us that a guest house a few doors up had another two rooms free.

We headed back to the conference centre to collect the others who were waiting to see the doctor and get their wounds treated.

Luke, Nathan and I, sat and watched Sky News for what seemed like hours. The footage was horrendous and I still didn't understand how we had managed to be so lucky. I watched the death toll climbing with a morbid fascination. Sky News reported that the estimated cost of the damage was running into billions of pounds. There were crowds of us watching in silence the images of huge waves in Thailand crashing onto the beaches. People were sitting on the floor, some injured, others crying. Each one of us found it hard to understand how we had survived. At this point they were reporting that the loss of human life was worse in Sri Lanka than elsewhere. Sri Lanka had been directly in the path of the tsunami. There was no news yet of Bande Ache.

This had been the second largest earthquake in history. The largest had been in Chile on 22 May, 1960. There the earthquake had been a magnitude of 9.5. This one was 9.0. The death toll stood at 50,000 and was expected to rise. Although I was not physically injured, coming to terms with this disaster was proving extremely difficult. Many of us just stood around in silence, jaws gaping, as we watched the television screens.

Because Colombo is a port, I still felt very vulnerable. Planes had been chartered to start flying people out. We had a family discussion about what we should do. Saskia and I desperately wanted to go home, but it seemed wrong for us to take up precious seats when there were so many injured and bereaved people that needed to get home quickly. My head was spinning and I wandered outside to get some fresh air.

Somebody grabbed my arm. It was Patricia the woman who had convinced me to help at The Rock. She was in a wheelchair. I smiled at her and she grasped my hand and said:

"You done well Tracey."

I didn't feel like I had, but I thanked her anyway. She had been the reason I pulled myself together in order to help and I was grateful for her stern words and rolling eyes.

I could tell Pat was upset about the prospect of us having to leave. This was his much awaited return to the land he had grown up in and he had been so excited. He pointed out that the country still needed the money from tourists and by staying we could be of some help. So we decided to head north to the hills and try to relax there instead of hanging around the airport for days getting more and more tired and nervous. It wasn't the best place to be, surrounded by all the images on the TV screens.

We went shopping for clothes at a big department store. Nathan had been wearing a woman's blouse for days – it was a shocking turquoise with flowers embroidered on it. He was relieved to be able to buy some T-shirts. We all laughed when a very camp store attendant asked Nathan where he had bought his shirt from. He actually liked it. If it hadn't been so dirty Nathan would have given it to him. We all came out with new wardrobes feeling much happier.

We stayed the night at our guest houses and in the morning we went back to the conference centre to sort out our travellers' cheques. Pat had his eyes tested for some new glasses. The optician said he had been watching the disaster unfold on television and had wanted to help. The only way he knew how was to bring his machines and offer his services to people who had lost their glasses in the tsunami. Pat received a nice new pair of spectacles. We bumped into lots of familiar faces at the centre. Some were heading north like us and others were booking flights home. I was happy to spot Neil and Andy sitting in the restaurant. We sat and chatted and arranged to meet for a beer at the Galle Face Hotel later that afternoon. Pat was going to hire an air conditioned minibus for the journey to Kandy the following day.

Our guest house had become a meeting point for the different organisations that had flown to Sri Lanka to start helping on the relief side of things. Camille told us she wanted to go back down south with them to help for a few days and meet us later in Kandy. I couldn't decide if she was being very brave or mad.

That evening, Luke, Nathan and I made our way to the Galle Face Hotel to meet Neil and Andy. They were sitting on the terrace. I was glad that they had chosen to sit there, as it was a higher level than the tables next to the sea where we had sat on our first night. We were all relieved to see one another. I ordered a Gin and Tonic and sat back in my chair. The happiness I had felt last time we were here was tarnished now. The sea looked different in my eyes. Not just something to admire but something to fear. The same waves I had enjoyed watching lapping against the rocks under the moonlight two weeks ago, now looked very different. We shared nervous jokes about being next to the sea and all agreed that the tsunami had changed our outlook on life. Every time a wave broke loudly we all raised our eyebrows together. We talked and talked for hours over our drinks, dissecting the horrors we had seen and experienced.

Another familiar face from The Rock appeared at the bar. He reminded me of John Lennon with long hair and small round glasses perched on the end of his nose. Coincidentally his name was John. He ordered a beer and joined us which gave us another excuse to talk about the tsunami again. It was cathartic for us all.

Then Andy and Neil had to split in order to catch their flights to Thailand and Australia. We said our goodbyes and promised to exchange photographs when we all got home. Although I had only known these guys for a few days I felt sad saying goodbye to them. Together we had kept one another sane during our time on The Rock. We were all concerned for Paul, as none of us had seen him since then. We knew he was alright but had no way of contacting him.

John's wife, Tanya, and their children, Jonah and Nat, joined us. They were the most grounded little kids I have ever met. When I asked them how they were, they talked about feeling stressed but they knew they would come to terms with it. They were young, and yet so mature. I hoped the tsunami hadn't stolen their innocence. I hoped that they were already like this. John and Tanya only stayed a short while before saying they had to get the kids to bed.

We waited for the rest of the family. When they arrived, we treated ourselves to the Sri Lankan buffet. Tables were spilling over with every kind of food. A nagging thought in the back of my head reminded me of the people we had left behind. I hoped they had enough food tonight.

I awoke in the night with a start. A loud roaring noise had disturbed me. I ran to the window in a panic but it was a false alarm. Luke jumped up, startled by me. I guessed it was a motor bike. Even in my sleep I was always expecting the worst, always on guard.

We woke early and packed our bags. We had breakfast in a little vegetarian place around the corner. I noticed a local man in his fifties watching us from across the room. He was using his fingers to feed himself. The more I tried not to look across at him the more we had eye contact. I smiled nervously. He got up from his chair and walked towards us and leant over our table.

"Be very careful my friends, I have heard there are more waves coming, much bigger," he said, and walked back to his table where he continued eating.

I gulped. Maybe he was psychic. Maybe he knew something we didn't. He continued to stare and I continued to catch his eye. I was worried but Pat and Fran convinced me that he was scaremongering. As we left, the man raised his eyebrows. He had unnerved me and as we walked back to our guest house to wait for our minibus, his words kept going around in my head.

22 – HEADING NORTH

We waited for our driver, getting agitated more by the minute. Pat reminded us we were in Sri Lanka. His Indian friend from Manchester always said that there is Atomic time, Sidereal time (timed by the sun) and Indian time. Five minutes can mean five hours or five days. Most Sri Lankans seemed to work on Indian time.

Reporters were milling around trying to get a gruesome story. Camille had decided to leave with the German group of rescue workers. They were heading south in a big truck with aid for the devastated zones.

The driver arrived at our guest house, two hours later than expected, to take us on our journey. A young man, clean shaven and dressed in a shirt too big for him, he approached us with a big smile. He said his name was Abdul. He didn't seem bothered by his lateness and had no idea why we looked so unhappy.

We loaded the vehicle and, hot and sweaty, climbed inside. At last we were heading to the safety of the hills, far away from the sea. We kissed Camille goodbye and told her that it wasn't too late for her to change her mind and jump in with us. But she was adamant that she was going back down south.

She left us clutching a stack of rolled up mattresses. Abdul started the engine and we all sniggered as it spluttered and groaned. We couldn't wait for the air conditioning to start up. The traffic in Colombo was stationary and the usual wild hooting of horns ensued. Tuk-tuks and motorbikes were weaving in and out of the cars. Sweat rolled down our faces and hair stuck to our foreheads as we breathed in the heavy car fumes of the busy city. The air conditioner only blew out hot air. We tried every conceivable way to get it to work. Windows closed, windows open, back windows open, front windows open, but with no joy. Abdul seemed delighted by the hot heat blowing in his face. He smiled and bobbed his head. Eventually, we gave up. We were like chickens cooking in an oven.

We opened the windows wide but the air outside was as hot and humid as that inside the bus. We were hardly moving so there was no chance of a breeze. We crawled through the busy roads and out of the city. I never like driving in Asia so sat rigidly in my seat, waiting for Abdul to slam his foot down on his accelerator. Sure enough, once out of traffic, with a screech we were off. We all gripped our seats and swung from side to side as he zigzagged in and out, swerving to avoid oncoming cars. Our hot sweaty bodies were the least of our worries now. I was not going to let him kill us in his old banger. Annoyed at his dangerous driving, I shouted at him to slow down, but he seemed to find this amusing. Our nerves frayed, we all shouted together and he finally slowed down.

We arrived in a small town and Abdul pulled over, telling us that he would be one minute. We sat in the van in the midday sun with children's faces staring in at us. After a ten minutes and no sign of Abdul, we decided to get off the bus to find some shade. We were all fed up by now. Ten minutes went by, then twenty, thirty. Fifty minutes later Abdul returned, smiling, with a carrier bag.

Pat remarked that we wanted to arrive in Kandy by day and not at night. Abdul's response was to speed off again to make up time. We all screamed. He slowed down, bobbing his head at us. We grimaced at one another. He was to be our driver for the next week.

The sun dropped and we were still some distance from Kandy. We weaved amongst the hills. I longed to take a shower and relax. Pat became excited as we approached Kegalle, the town in which he had grown up. He pointed out various landmarks as if he had lived here yesterday. I felt sad that this long anticipated trip had become more about the tsunami than Pat's past. I looked out of my window and imagined Pat as a small boy here. It intrigued me how very different his childhood had been to mine.

The signs told us that we were close to Kandy. The roads were lined with white triangular flags instead of the usual multi coloured Buddhist flags. Abdul got lost so we went around and around for ages, before Pat recognised a street junction and told Abdul to turn left. To our amazement we were on the right road. Despite the years, this place remained ingrained in his memory. Pat's happiness was visible. He was leaning casually out of the window, looking around curiously, with a big smile.

Set amongst gorgeous rolling hills and tea plantations, Kandy is built around a lake and is Sri Lanka's second biggest city. It's culturally vibrant and bursting with colonial remnants including Dutch Forts, canals, churches, British residences, clubs and courthouses. The Sri Dalada Maligawa Temple is home to the relic of the sacred tooth of Buddha.

Trying to find our guest house turned into another fiasco. We drove round and round the lake until my head was spinning. We had spent hours in the van and badly needed to get out. Finally Abdul found "Sunray". We all climbed out of the bus and stretched. It felt good to be standing at last. The house was lavish with marble floors and all the bedrooms had balconies. Although, we were high in the hills, I was relieved to see that they were on the first floor.

The tropical jungle plants formed a canopy over the entrance. The friendly owners walked down to the reception to greet us. Two young boys were giggling and whispering to one another. The owner snapped at them in Sinhalese and they ran towards us to carry our luggage. They smiled with big, wide mouths and said hello before running ahead excitedly with our bags to show us to our rooms. They were clean with comfortable beds. Maybe now we could relax, I thought. Pat tipped the young lads with a handful of rupees and they were ecstatic. Grinning from ear to ear, they ran off.

Abdul's next blag was to inform us that we also had to pay for his accommodation. He stood there looking all forlorn with a carrier bag containing his clothes for the week. I remember shuddering, thinking he couldn't have bought enough pants with him. Pat asked the owner if this was the case and, after shouting at Abdul in Sinhalese, he told us that the car hire company had already paid for him. Abdul pulled a childish face which made us laugh as he sloped off.

We were quite high up so it was chilly and drizzling, but the guest house boasted hot showers. When I walked into the bathroom I shrieked with horror, not at the two frogs in the sink, but the actual shower. Wires from the mains were hanging loosely under the shower head. All the showers were the same. Pat advised showering under cold water and told us a story about an author named Thomas Merton who had been fatally electrocuted in a shower in Sri Lanka. I listened to Pat and made my decision right there. Cold it was. Around every corner, it seemed, we were dicing with death again.

Luke decided to take the risk and have a hot shower. He made me stand there with the plastic handle of my hairbrush sticking into the wall switch. I was instructed to quickly switch it off if he got electrocuted, although I couldn't see what good that would do, after the event.

When we were all showered, we headed into town. Nathan recalled that Stuart, from The Rock, had told him to visit The Pub if we made it to Kandy. Despite the uninspiring name, the bar was very welcoming after our long journey. We ordered cold beers and a bottle of wine and the Chardonnay arrived in an ice bucket.

"CHEERS to Stuart!" We smiled as our glasses clinked together. Taking our first gulps, sinking back into our chairs, our shared relief was apparent. As the breeze, created by the electric fans, blew on our hot faces we began to unwind.

We were able to make phone calls to family and friends and could talk leisurely here. I spoke to my mum and sister. Back at home people had managed to contact one another. Luke's auntie Roz had got in touch with my family after endless hours of ringing London Zoo. Sue, a family friend house-sitting in Wandsworth, had despaired about trying to contact Fran's sister. She had searched everywhere for her number until she saw an invite to Roz's fiftieth birthday party pinned on the notice board.

A Times' reporter had been snooping around the neighbourhood looking for a story: FAMILY OF EIGHT PERISH IN TSUNAMI. He had been in local pubs, knocking on doors and constantly ringing the family home. Sadly, he didn't want to run a story that we had all survived.

When Jim died at the zoo I remember how the reporters arrived like swarms of flies. Not caring for our grief, but just wanting their gruesome story. The reporters would hover around waiting to shove a microphone in our faces with no respect for Jim or us. Now, I learned that the Wandsworth Borough News had run a story reporting that we were missing, causing panic and upset for all who knew us.

My sister Dawn told me that she had phoned the zoo. My boss Malcolm had chatted with her and they had tried to convince one another that we were ok. Malcolm, a very kind Scotsman with a big heart, became the link for friends all over the country and kept everyone informed. Although unsure himself over our fate, he remained positive.

Dawn then told me how she had received the phone call everyone had been waiting for. She had lifted the receiver to her ear to hear, "Happy Christmas!" from Andy from the zoo. Dawn hesitated before wishing Andy a Happy Christmas.

"THEY'RE ALIVE!" shouted Andy.

Dawn had collapsed on the floor. Andy explained that he had received our text. He had called Linda's mobile number to try and talk to us but was told to get off the line and not to ring again. The news travelled like wildfire to friends up and down the country and around the world. Many people later told me that they had gone out that evening and celebrated.

After we finished our calls, we needed to eat. The Pub's dining room had a huge screen with twenty-four hour news of the disaster blaring out. It was the same images of dead bodies and waves that we had watched in Colombo. Tourists were glued to the screen. No matter how much we tried to engage in conversation, our eyes would drift back. Saskia went to e-mail Camille to let her know where we were staying. She was going to come and find us after she had finished distributing aid with the German relief workers.

Our meals arrived and tears flowed down my face. I tried to hide my sadness from the rest of the group, but Luke and Fran noticed and kept talking to me, while they ate, avoiding eye contact to spare me any embarrassment. The more I tried to stifle my tears and sobs the worse they became. This trauma had no pattern to it. One minute I was laughing and the next my tears started again. I wanted to get a plane home but I knew that there were people who needed the seats more than us. At the same time, I wanted to see Pat's childhood home and not to spoil things for him by asking to leave. So I pulled myself together and tried to enjoy the evening.

The next day Luke and I decided to travel up to Pinnawala Elephant Orphanage. We had a special reason for going there. Geetha, one of our lovely elephants from London Zoo, had come from the orphanage in 1982. She had been found by some locals stuck in a water hole and abandoned by her mother. She was traumatised and half starved. They managed to pull her out with great effort and the help of their water buffalos and ropes. Geetha was taken to the orphanage and lived there until a home was found for her at London Zoo. A keeper had travelled out to Sri Lanka to work with her at the orphanage and get to know her. When Geetha was two years old she came to London with him. After Jim's death, she was moved to Whipsnade Wild Animal Park with our other two- Mya and Azizah.

We met the curator at the orphanage and he showed us around. He remembered Geetha and was excited by our connection. The orphanage is home to many elephants which mean a lot of cleaning for the staff. There seemed to be plenty of *mahouts* who undertook a variety of jobs. When we arrived, a vet was treating one of the elephants.

The curator shouted over to him and pointed excitedly at us talking away in Sinhalese. The vet smiled enthusiastically and waved. I could see that he was proud to be showing us around. The *mahouts* were having terrible trouble trying to control the beast as the vet waited patiently, ready with an injection to push into the elephant's thick leathery skin. They were all pulling on chains and shouting commands in Sinhalese. I recognised some of the commands from working with Geetha.

"Pitchit," they were shouting, which means "stop it," and "medaha," which means "come here". The large pachyderm was not keen to obey. As the vet forced the sharp needle into his skin, the elephant let out an almighty roar of disparagement, which made me jump.

The lush vegetation and banana plants made a beautiful tropical backdrop. There was a wide river running along the edge of the orphanage where a herd of elephants were being washed by their *mahouts*. Jim had travelled here once. I had seen photos of him in the river with his trousers rolled up washing a baby elephant. I smiled to myself as I reminisced about times gone by. I was surprised that the smell of elephant dung filling the air was so familiar and comforting. I was not unnerved by the elephants at all, but felt a healthy respect for them. People were holding their noses and laughing, but I breathed in deeply, closed my eyes and enjoyed the pungent aroma. I must have filled around three thousand skips of elephant dung during my time working with them.

We spent a relaxing morning at the orphanage and thanked the curator for his hospitality. He gave us his business card and said he looked forward to seeing us in London. We then set off to find Pat and the rest of the family.

23 – GOLLINDA, KEGALLE

It was now our turn to drive Abdul mad. We climbed into our hot sweaty bus and headed into the hills towards Kegalle. Tea grows well here as it needs a warm climate, the right altitude and a sloping terrain. This is exactly what the Sri Lankan countryside offers. In the distance I could see the tea pickers. I could tell that they were women by their colourful dress. They had large, round, wicker baskets on their backs to fill with tea leaves. It reminded me of the painting on Thalik's wall in Unawatuna. We were looking for the Gollinda plantation where Pat had grown up. Round and round the hills we went and kept driving into dead ends, and Abdul's reversing on hillsides was not good for our nerves.

Pat had a feeling that we were close. We stopped to ask some curious villagers for directions to Gollinda. They were more interested in why a van of white people was up here. Smiling faces looked through the windows. The little girls eyed our jewellery, knocked on the glass and chatted excitedly to one another. When we smiled back, they hid shyly behind their mother's dresses pulling them over their faces. The old men chatted with Abdul and pointed us in the right direction. We waved goodbye and they waved enthusiastically at us. Abdul's patience was clearly starting to fray. He sighed heavily, his shoulders dropping in despair, as he turned the key in the ignition. Off we went again.

I was starting to wonder if Pat would be able to find his old house. But over another hill and the surroundings began to feel more familiar to him. I watched as he concentrated, tapping his knee with his fingers.

"Go right here," he suddenly instructed Abdul.

Abdul took the right turn along a dirt track. There on the side of the road was a small metal sign, Gollinda. He had found it. We followed the road as it hugged the hillside and there on the left was a small building.

"That was my father's office," Pat said, smiling.

He asked Abdul to stop. I climbed out with him, glad to be able to stretch my legs. We walked down some old rickety steps, brushing away cobwebs, and peered through the dirty window. A sign was hanging off a metal post painted green and white. "Office" I rubbed the glass with my hand to get a better look and there inside was an old desk with an old fashioned rubber stamp on it. There was a safe in the corner and paper work piled up. It felt as if time had stood still and his father had just popped out, away from his desk. The office seemed to have been kept a secret all these years, hidden away amongst the tea plantations. For Pat it was exactly as he remembered. Excitedly, he pointed to various items of furniture, and I could hear the emotion in his voice. This was truly incredible.

"Shit," he whispered, "amazing."

I took a photo of Pat underneath the old office sign. I giggled to myself at the sweat patches all over Pat's lovely lilac shirt but he had no change of clothes in the van for the photo shoot so it was either that or topless.

Pat wanted to carry on driving to try and find his house. We returned to the vehicle and drove further up the hill leaving the office behind us. I am very nostalgic and if it had been my family's office I would have liked to touch everything and stay for longer, sit in the chair, remembering the past and the people that were once here but Pat was eager to continue. He was like an excited child on Christmas morning.

The scenery was amazing. The lush green hills were dotted with banana plants as huge as the conifers in England. It was humid and the van was stifling. We approached a small road which had low brick walls either side.

"This is it," said Pat, "This is it, we are here."

Abdul looked relieved as he pulled over and put his handbrake on with a loud sigh. Everybody got out and looked around, stretching, and breathing in the fresh, clean air. Pat had grown up surrounded by these rolling hills and beautiful trees. There were flocks of Orange-billed babblers and Blossom-headed parakeets sitting in the trees chattering, their shrieks pierced our ears. Apart from that, it was silent, no distant rumble of traffic, nothing.

The pathway to Pat's house was overgrown with the lush vegetation. Specimen plants and brightly coloured flowers pushed their heads through the dense foliage. Pat's mother had planted these herself and they had grown and spread over the years. Pat and Luke decided to try and make their way through the undergrowth, but the rest of us were worried about snakes so we hung back. As we waited, we could hear them crashing through the undergrowth, hacking back the foliage with sticks, desperate for a glimpse of Pat's old home.

They couldn't find the house. Pat knew it was the same path and was disappointed that the house was no longer there. At least he could see the flowers and travel back in time, briefly remembering the long, winding path of his childhood and his father returning home from the office. We left him alone as he stood with his hands on his hips and soaked up the familiar surroundings, looking out across the hills, remembering his past.

"Right lets go and celebrate," said Pat. After all, it was New Year's Eve.

So we all climbed back into the hot sticky van with its broken air conditioning. We sat quietly, each of us lost in our own thoughts of how we would feel if we were Pat. Abdul told us that he was starving and was desperate to leave. We had forgotten that he hadn't eaten a thing all day and probably thought we were mad coming all this way to look at an old office and watch Pat and Luke climb through the undergrowth.

We arrived back in Kandy and the streets were lined with white flags. Abdul told us that it was a national day of mourning for the victims of the tsunami. He pulled up outside our hotel and looked relieved to be getting rid of us.

The man on the desk said we had a visitor and to our delight we saw Camille walking towards us. Thank god she was safe. Camille had travelled back down south, stopping at villages and handing out aid to the ever thankful Sri Lankans. She witnessed again the devastation the tsunami had left behind. Camille described to us how they had taken a lorry load of mattresses, medical supplies and drinking water to the survivors. She explained that although people needed everything, mattresses were the most important to them as sleeping outside on rubble was so distressing. They needed to sleep properly in order to function normally. I had graphic images in my head as I recalled trying to sleep on the concrete. I now had a bed, but the survivors were still in the same situation as when we boarded our buses. They had started to head further south when a news flash came over the radio that another tsunami was on the way. Feeling vulnerable Camille decided she couldn't go any further and wanted to be with her family. She stopped the lorry driver and explained that she didn't want to continue with them, that she had seen enough the first time round. It was time to call it a day. She left the group and got a lift back north to Colombo with some locals.

Once safely back in Colombo, she'd learned that the reports of more waves had been false. The Indian government had erroneously announced this information causing panic throughout Asia. But she booked her train to Kandy to join us anyway. We all listened to her story and were glad she had made the right decision. She looked tired and needed to unwind.

We decided to go and see the Buddha's tooth and strolled into town. I could not believe how many people were queuing to get into the temple. It was New Year and there were thousands wanting to say prayers for the victims of the tsunami. We joined the queue and about an hour later, barefoot and sweating, swayed with the crowds into the temple. Outside I heard the familiar sound of an ice-cream van, playing the same tune as the one on the beach in Unawatuna. Luke recognised the tune too and held my hand.

I needed to get out of the temple, it was all too much. The crowds and sadness were overwhelming. I wanted to be alone with my grief. I stumbled out and, breathing fresh air, felt better. As I sat and waited for the rest of the family, I watched thousands of candles burning and said a silent prayer.

A bull elephant with his face chalked up and flowers draped around his neck made me smile. I watched as people touched his forehead then his trunk whilst saying a prayer. He looked unimpressed and lifted a woman's sari with his trunk as she walked off, flashing her knickers. She screamed, distraught, while everyone around her laughed. The elephant handler ran and hit the poor beast with his ankus but he didn't flinch. His wise eyes looked ahead as his big jaw chewed the food in his mouth. People kept putting flowers on his head which he instantly shook off by flapping his huge ears. He looked bored with the attention and chewed on the banana leaves the *mahout* had placed on the floor for him.

Luke's family came out and we decided to go back to The Pub for a beer. It was unusually quiet so we were thrilled to get a big table. The waiter approached us and we began to order "one bottle of white wine and..." but he stopped us in our tracks.

"Sorry, we serve no alcohol for three days."

We must have looked like raging alcoholics as we questioned why. We needed a drink to celebrate Camille's safe return and New Year's Eve and just life. The waiter looked at us and explained that Sri Lanka had declared three days of national mourning. Suddenly, we felt awful and as I looked around at the tables occupied by tourists it was obvious that everybody was drinking coffee or orange juice. I was so embarrassed.

Although we understood and respected this period of mourning, the devil jumps onto your shoulder. We needed a drink to help us cope with what we had been through. So instead of staying for a coffee we skulked off sheepishly to find somewhere else. We found an old bar around the corner, Pub Royale, which was serving alcohol. We couldn't understand why they were allowed to serve us, regardless of what the rest of Sri Lanka was doing, but were grateful for our drinks. The building was beautiful, very old, and in need of some love and attention. The bar staff were all elderly men dressed in crisp white shirts and smart red waist coats. They were clearly proud of their bar and polished the heavy, dark wooden tables over and over again. I sat with my drink and although I tried very hard to put the tsunami behind me I was finding it increasingly difficult to unwind. I needed to go home but was wracked with guilt at the thought of spoiling the remainder of Pat's trip.

I kept drifting off unable to concentrate on conversation. Saskia confided in me that she wanted to get a flight home. She was worried about the books she had been lost in the wave and how the university would react. She also wanted to see her boyfriend and friends. I agreed that I wanted to get home too. We told the rest of the family and Fran suggested we call the airport the next day. Pat was very gracious and didn't try to stop us from leaving. He understood our reasons, but I knew he was disappointed.

Everywhere was now closed in Kandy and there was nowhere to have our supper, so we headed back to our hotel to see in the New Year. They had food and a bar. But of course when we arrived back they weren't selling alcohol and the kitchen was closed. We were so hungry that they offered to do us some rice and gave us two bottles of beer between the eight of us. Although grateful for their kindness, it was a depressing New Year's Eve. We counted down 10, 9, 8, 7, 6, 5, 4, 3, 2, and 1, laughed and clinked our glasses each with a mouthful of beer. We then said a prayer for all those who had died and went to bed. I never like celebrating the New Year as I worry about what it might bring but this time I was glad to be alive.

Luke chatted with me and said it would be good if I could stay just a few more days as it was easier to get one flight for Saskia rather than two. I pondered and agreed.

A new day began and our goal was to get Saskia onto a plane and home to England. Fran rang the airport and found a flight for Saskia to leave first thing the next morning. This meant returning to Colombo to catch her flight so Fran and Pat decided to travel overnight with her and meet up with us in Kandy the following day.

That evening, we took Saskia out for a farewell dinner. She was happy to be leaving Sri Lanka. She collected her bag and we said our goodbyes.

24 – TIME TO GO

We went to bed and I couldn't sleep. I was restless and wished that I had left with Saskia. I kept thinking how lucky she was. Although I had tried to put the tsunami behind me, it was becoming increasingly difficult to pretend that I was feeling ok. I really needed to go home. It was difficult to feel safe and no matter how high up in the hills we were, I still felt vulnerable. When it rained, I imagined mud slides.

I woke to the sounds of monkeys bouncing around on the balcony and so I got up to watch them. They were hysterical little toque macaques creating havoc. I laughed as they beat one another up and pulled the washing off the line. They used telephone cables to get from A to B and were very mischievous.

I decided to wait for Luke to wake up and then to phone the airport. I was worried they would make me wait until my actual return date, as I hadn't boarded one of the earlier chartered planes put on for survivors. After he'd showered, I told him my plan and he insisted on coming home with me. We called the airport and were told to ring back in the afternoon when they would have a better idea of available seats. Pat and Fran arrived back from Colombo. Saskia was now thirty-five thousand feet in the sky heading home.

Abdul had apparently had enough of us. A new chauffeur had driven them back to Kandy. Yappa was more mature. He wore a pair of smart cream trousers and a cream shirt. His hair was wavy and greased and he enjoyed combing it, even when he was driving and puffing on a cigarette. His aroma filled the bus – a mixture of stale fags and BO.

Afternoon came and we called the airport again. They told Luke they had only one seat. I felt exhausted, but Luke persisted and in the end we were told that they could get us both on a flight together in a couple of days.

We had time on our hands so agreed to see a bit more of the country. We decided to travel to Anuradhapura and visit the Dambulla caves and a rock palace called Sigiriya. Yappa patiently followed our directions to the Nimnara Lake Resort. The rooms were situated on the edge of the lake and the sky was full of rich birdlife. The rooms were luxurious and clean with hot power-showers. It was run by a large, motherly woman. She showed us her guest book and explained that since the tsunami all her booked guests had cancelled. For the local people, tourism is their main source of income so we were glad to be of some help. We spent the rest of the day relaxing in the tropical grounds of her home and in the evening enjoyed a feast fit for kings.

The following day we ambled around the countryside. The Dambulla caves are thought to date back to the first century BC when King Valagambahu was driven out of the capital, Anuradhapura, and took refuge there. It was a steep walk up steps carved into the rock and about 150 metres above the main road. There were monkeys running around everywhere and we were asked to remove our shoes. The ground was baking, it was like walking on hot coals, and we yelped as we darted from the shaded areas across the scorching rock. There were five different caves to explore and every one took my breath away. Each of the carved interiors contained about one hundred and fifty Buddha images. The colours were so vibrant that the murals looked as if they had been painted that morning.

Our next stop was Sigiriya. It stands alone, 370 metres above sea level, and can be seen from miles around; a gigantic rock poking through the jungle. It took us about an hour and a half to reach the top. For the last bit of the climb we had to use a rickety metal staircase. It was a hair-raising experience for us all. The top of the rock is 1.6 hectares. It was incredible to think that once this would have been a vibrant palace with market stalls. The king's throne, carved into the stone, was still there and I felt very privileged to stand where he had over 1500 years ago, surveying his kingdom. I sat on his stone throne to admire the palace. The views across the jungle were spectacular and the whole experience made me feel utterly insignificant.

Sri Lanka's classical architecture, sculpture and painting are predominantly Buddhist. There are stupas or dagobas, Buddhist monuments containing relics of the Buddha or a Buddhist saint, all over the country and several Buddha sculptures which take your breath away.

We went to explore the vast city ruins of Anuradhapura which went on for miles. Noisy troupes of toque macaques marched around, intimidating the tourists by pulling menacing faces and flashing their teeth. Even the babies on their mothers' backs joined in by squeaking at the tourists. It was obviously a game that had been played for generations.

Hanuman langurs bounded around harassing the stall owners and stealing any food they could. Their slender frames, speed and agility put paid to any two-legged human catching them with their loot. Their long, silvery coats shimmered in the sunlight as they bounced and ran with shiny black faces, sweat on their brows, their long feet and hands slapping on the rock.

The langurs are believed to be incarnations of the Hindu Monkey God, Hanuman, who, legend has it, fought to rescue a queen from a forest fire. He got caught in the fire on his heroic dash and burned his face, hands and back feet, hence the black hands and feet against their silver coats.

We had some on my section at London Zoo and it fascinated me to see the wild ones behave in a similar fashion to our captive ones. They are also thieves and steal the sloth bears' food by jumping around to distract them and then grabbing whatever is in their bowls. Before the bears have time to register what's happened they are gone with their food.

We went to see the Jaya Sri Maha Bodhi, a sacred fig tree, bought over from India by a princess who introduced the Buddha's teaching to Sri Lanka. The Bodhi tree is where the Buddha sat when he attained enlightenment. The shape of the overturned leaf is said to have inspired the shape of the Buddhist Temple. This particular tree has been tended religiously for over two thousand years. Multi-coloured prayer flags were draped over the ruins around the tree. There were people praying next to offerings of food and candles. The air was full of the scent of thousands of joss sticks burning.

Another farewell meal was planned. I packed my bag and felt relieved to be on the move. At dinner, we all reflected on our trip to Sri Lanka. Apart from the tsunami, I had really enjoyed seeing this beautiful and enchanting island.

The minibus arrived and we climbed on board and waved from our windows. I felt a strange mix of emotions. I worried that I had disappointed Pat and that we were letting down the people of Sri Lanka by not staying in their country, deserting them when they needed our custom more than ever. But it also felt right to be leaving. Although family and friends knew that we were alive, they would still be worried and want to see and touch us to know for sure that we were ok.

Yappa turned on the ignition and off we screeched. Colombo was a few hours away. It was a humid evening and the bus was warm. I looked out of the window and watched the hills with their twinkling lights darken against the deep navy sky. The roads were lined with tropical vegetation and street stalls, with women cooking food in big frying pans. The smell of garlic filled the bus. People hung around along the roadside chatting and eating.

The road was more like a dirt track and had gigantic pot holes which, together with the erratic driving, made for an uncomfortable ride. We bounced up and down and I gave up counting how many times my head smacked the ceiling.

Luke had fallen asleep. I watched headlights on full beam race towards us and at the last minute both vehicles would swerve and miss a head on collision. The driving in Sri Lanka is like a synchronized dance. Everyone seems aware of their space and place as they glide in and out, narrowly missing one another. Lorries kept speeding towards us through the dark night, their loud horns bursting my eardrums and shattering my nerves.

Watching Yappa in his rear view mirror, I could see he looked sleepy and he kept shutting his eyes.

I started tapping him on his shoulder and asking him questions to make sure he was not drifting off. This was my mission for the rest of the journey. I could see he was irritated and he kept yawning, but I didn't care. At last there were signs for Colombo and the airport. I woke Luke as we came to a screeching standstill at the airport terminal and we grabbed our rucksacks and climbed out.

The airport was packed and we had a few hours to kill. Aware that we were by the sea again I opted to sit upstairs in the waiting area. We only had enough money left for one bottle of water so we sipped it sparingly. With early morning, more airport staff started to arrive. We went to pick up our tickets from the desk. The flight attendants led me into a room and started chatting to one another and laughing.

"Were you there then madam?" asked a middle-aged man.

"Yes," I replied.

The table was suddenly surrounded by airline staff in smart, navy blue uniforms. One wanted to know the size of the wave. Another asked how many bodies I had seen. It was surreal. They didn't seem to care about what had happened to the victims, they just wanted to hear grisly details. I was shocked. All I could see were lips endlessly mouthing questions at me. I hadn't slept the night before and began to feel faint.

"Can I please have our tickets?" I asked, too exhausted to answer their repetitive questioning. The door swung open and a stern looking woman walked in. They all scurried back to their desks. She ignored me but after talking to them she turned like a praying mantis and smiled at me.

"Can I help you?" she asked.

"Yes please. I have reserved tickets to collect," I replied.

"Oh, why is that?" she asked.

"Because we have brought our flights forward" All the people in the office were looking at us.

"Haven't you enjoyed Sri Lanka then?" she asked.

"Yes, we loved the country, it's very beautiful," I said, starting to lose my patience. "Do you have our tickets please?"

"Yes, we do. Ah, here they are. So did you see the tsunami?" she asked.

I snapped. "Yes we did, it was awful, a lot of people have died and the ones who survived have nothing left. They lost everything they owned and often their whole family."

She handed me the tickets and wished me a safe journey. None of the staff had shown any concern for the loss of precious lives in their country. The tsunami seemed just to be a source of some cheap gossip for them.

I went into the toilets and saw my reflection in the mirror. I looked old and haunted. I splashed cold water on my face, slapped and pinched my cheeks and ran some water through my hair before giving up. I remembered Paul teasing me about my appearance at The Rock. This was a repeat of that face, minus the running mascara.

We boarded our plane. I sat by the window, put on my seat belt and pulled it tight. The hot morning sun was beating down on the runway. I held Luke's hand as the pilot fired up the engines and taxied into position. I hate take-off so my palms started sweating and I squeezed Luke's hand tightly which made him yelp.

The huge roaring of the engines and the force of the plane as we raced down the runway got my adrenalin running. I felt the plane start to lift and we were airborne. The loud clunk of the landing gear folding away made me stop breathing for a minute, and then I sighed: We were heading home.

I looked out of the window and there was the sea, washing gently onto golden stretches of sand, lined with palms. I could see the white of the waves as they broke on the sand. Tears started to prick my eyes. I turned my back on Luke so he wouldn't see. As the plane curved on its side, I watched the sun catch its wing as the coastline of Sri Lanka disappeared from my view.

25 – ARRIVING BACK IN ENGLAND

As we started our descent over the sea, I could see England all lush and green. I felt a weird sense of comfort even though I was still in this big metal bird and not safely on the ground yet. The plane's wheels gently bumped onto the runway and I grabbed the arms of my seat and pushed my right foot hard on the floor as if helping the pilot to brake. The engines roared into reverse and I remembered the roar of the tsunami. I was so relieved to be back on the ground and home in good old Blighty. As usual, everyone jumped up out of their seats, pushing and grabbing at the overhead luggage containers, before being told to sit back down.

Two police officers entered the cabin and I instantly thought it was something to do with terrorism. We sat and waited while they talked with the flight attendants. Then they called out and asked for anybody who had been in the areas hit by the tsunami to raise their hands. I was surprised that there were so few of us. One of them leant over and handed us a form to fill in, asking if we had lost any friends or relatives. At that moment I was so grateful to be able to say no, that we had all survived. It was strangely comforting to have British policemen in their smart, clean uniforms chatting with us. Finally, I felt safe.

As we waited for our baggage I imagined those people who would have had a very different story for the police officers a week ago. I hoped they had been as caring to the bereaved as they had been to us.

It was freezing outside and I felt stupid getting on the tube in my flip-flops. I didn't even have a tan.

We headed back to Wandsworth where Saskia was waiting, having prepared a meal for us. She looked much happier than when I had last seen her in Sri Lanka and we were happy to be reunited. One of the wounds on her feet had gone septic. It looked black and she said that she had been experiencing pain in her legs and lower back. We advised her to go to hospital first thing in the morning to avoid a blood infection. Before ordering a taxi home, I rang Mum and she told me that she would be down with Dawn the following morning.

I felt exhilarated as I put the key in our front door and the cats, Frank and Mindy, ran to greet us. We picked them up and cuddled them. It was good to be home. All the familiar things and smells made me feel safe. We dropped our rucksacks to the floor and switched on the television to see the news.

The first image was of a baby and as the reporter started to talk my blood ran cold. It was Baby Harry. His granddad, an actor from *The Bill*, was talking about him. We both sat in silence, with tears running down our cheeks. Baby Harry was the youngest British victim of the tsunami. I couldn't believe that we were watching the first body we had seen in the disaster.

We then watched film footage of the Queen of the Sea, her carriages on their side or upside down. The bars on the windows made me shudder. We had been on that very train a few weeks earlier and had passed the destroyed railway track on our way back to Colombo. Now we were here in London looking at the pictures on our telly.

We turned off the television. I wanted to have a good soak. In the bath, I moved the water around and imagined how the earthquake had created the waves. The slightest movement caused ripples but if I punched the water I created waves.

Friends had called and arranged a reunion at our local pub. We wrapped up and strolled down there. I looked through the window and saw Malcolm and Jackie sitting at a big table that they had reserved for everybody. Mal ordered Champagne and friends started arriving. It was wonderful to see them all again. We cried and laughed, as we chatted, until the bell rang for last orders. We all went home grateful to have one another. I awoke several times during the night in a panic and was relieved to find myself safe in my bed in London. We got up early to wait for Mum and Dawn.

I was grateful that the zoo had offered me compassionate leave on my return. Our Human Resources Department was exceptionally kind and told me to see how I felt in a couple of weeks. Although not physically hurt, I still felt weepy and disturbed by the whole experience.

My mum and sister came to stay and I was so happy to see them. My poor mum just kept staring at me. She looked worn-out and tired. Dawn whispered to me in the kitchen that she had been in a terrible way and deeply affected by it all. So we just stayed in and talked which helped us all feel better.

Dawn told me she had heard that the government was giving free counselling to victims and survivors of the tsunami. I told Luke but he had no interest. He was no stranger to disaster and accidents and was more resilient than me. I was slightly apprehensive but decided to give it a go. After Jim died, my doctor had set me up with a counsellor and it was an awful experience. She was a brusque South African woman who told me that my main problem was that I was a man hater and that this was why I was so affected by Jim's death. I was so shocked I got up and told her that my head was ok and that maybe she was the one who needed a shrink. I just needed somebody to talk things over with that had no connection with me.

The counselling Dawn had recommended was organised by The British Red Cross. I started to call around and kept hitting brick walls. Nobody seemed to know anything about it. Four hours later, I got through to a helpful woman, Edith Westley, who was very kind and over the next few days managed to set me up with a counsellor. She put me in touch with a wonderful woman, Jayne Shackman, who offered support and listened to me for hours. I received six hours of free help over the telephone which helped me immensely. She was a good listener and offered invalid advice. My main concern was that there would be a knock on effect from Jim's death at the zoo. I had just turned the corner after this tragedy and started to feel on the mend, only to walk into the tsunami. She reassured me that what I had experienced after Jim's death would be helpful rather than negative. The panic, upset, fear and chaos were all normal, she told me. The feelings I was experiencing now were protective rather than about to trigger the old trauma I had dealt with before. I was relieved to know this.

One of the most important things I remember her saying to me was that I had two choices –

to become a victim or a survivor. I chose the second. She told me to write down my feelings about what had happened in Sri Lanka, to help me digest the horrors I had seen, which I started to do almost obsessively. I would sit up until the early hours of the morning most nights tapping away on the computer.

26 – SEARCHING FOR DAMMIKA

Being off work also gave me the time to try and find Dammika and to trawl through websites of the missing, hoping to find a picture of the woman on the bench so that I could contact her family and tell them what I knew. I sat for hours reading other survivors' personal accounts, hoping one would lead me to Dammika but they never did. I found phone numbers for The Rock, The Village Inn, Sunil's Restaurant and various other hotels. I rang the numbers, but the lines were all dead. For days, I would call these numbers every few hours in the hope that the telephone lines had been restored but they never were.

I decided to send a letter to Dammika as we owed him money and I wanted to try and help. I thought about what to write and then got a pen and paper. In huge capital letters I wrote:

DAMMIKA, WE WANT TO HELP YOU.

WE OWE YOU MONEY AND NEED TO FIND YOU.

DO YOU REMEMBER US? WE WERE ON THE FIRST FLOOR OF YOUR GUEST HOUSE.

PLEASE CONTACT US.

TRACEY LEE AND LUKE WARREN

I included our address and telephone number and a photo of Luke to help him remember us. I put what I thought was his address on the envelope.

DAMMIKA, THE VILLAGE INN, UNAWATUNA, SRI LANKA

I went to the post box, kissed the envelope and prayed that it would find him. I was thrilled with my ingenious plan and couldn't wait to tell Luke. When he got home I excitedly told him what I had done. I was surprised when he looked at me blankly.

"What's up?" I asked Luke, with a puzzled expression.

"The letter could fall into the wrong hands and somebody could pretend to be him," said Luke.

I hadn't thought of that.

"Oh well too late now, it's on its way. Oh, and I included a photo of you." I waited.

"Why did you put a photo of me in there?" Luke asked, looking distressed.

"Because you are the better looking one of us," I laughed.

Luke shook his head and walked into the garden.

Every morning I waited for a phone call or a letter. I would wait for the postman and be disappointed. The second post would come and still no news. I kept trying the numbers but they were still dead.

I never found a picture of the woman on the bench posted on the websites for the missing. I searched for weeks looking through photos over and over again and still occasionally do now. I carry this story with me to this day. I could have given her family some closure and it might have helped them in their grief if they had been told what happened to her and that she had looked peaceful in death.

Everyone was safely back in England now and Duncan had returned to Japan. Luke and I arranged to go to Wandsworth for dinner. When we arrived at the house it was strange to see everyone in winter clothes Fran's foot had gone septic like Saskia's and they had been to the hospital to have their wounds treated. They were lucky to catch the infection in time and were both on antibiotics. Fran's whole leg was swollen, the skin stretched thin and showing her veins. We were all pleased to see one another in a safe environment. Pat and Fran were keen to tell us about the last part of their trip.

They had gone back to Pat's house with Yappa and some locals had suggested that they visit, The Gentlemen's Club, as some of the old men might remember his family. There, on the wall of the club, was an old photograph of Pat with his brother Robert and all their classmates. It had hung there for the past fifty odd years. Pat was over the moon as he sat down with an old Sri Lankan man who remembered Pat and Robert's father. They had a few beers and chatted for the whole afternoon. This encounter made Pat's trip. The elderly chap told Pat that his childhood home had been burnt down during the civil war in 1983.

There was a nice surprise in store for Saskia when Fran handed her a small parcel. She opened it slowly and squealed with delight to find her favourite silver bangle, shining and polished. Pat and Fran had met up with Thalik in Kandy after we had left. He had given them the number of his relatives in the north and when he arrived, they arranged to meet at the Queen's Hotel in Kandy. While cleaning up the Zimmer Rest, he had dug up Saki's bangle from the mud in her room and cleaned it and wrapped it up for her. It was an emotional reunion.

He also had a letter for Camille from Peter, the man we had tried to help get into his house. She had described him in great detail and left some money with Thalik to give to Peter if he could find him. Thalik had made it his mission to find this man and hand over the money. Thalik never ceased to amaze us with his kindness and honesty. Peter's note was very sweet and he thanked Camille from the bottom of his heart. We were all humbled that a man who had lost everything, all of his family, could muster up the energy to write a note. We sat and remembered him with great sadness. He had lost his entire family, young and old.

Pat recalled visiting his baby brother's grave, which was a shock to me, as I had always thought it was just him and Robert. They had been driving around Nuwara Eliya, where Pat had gone to school, and he had instantly recognised a cemetery. He asked Yappa to pull over and out of the blue told Fran that he had had a little brother, Andrew, and that he was buried there. Despite it being overgrown and unkempt, he knew exactly where the grave was situated. As a child, Pat told us, he had been fascinated by his baby brother's grave and used to play around it for hours.

Sadly, they couldn't find where his mother was buried. They searched everywhere until it became clear to Pat that he wasn't going to find her grave. He had become resigned to the fact that on this trip it would not be possible but he promised himself he would find her next time. Despite the tsunami, Pat derived a lot of comfort from revisiting these childhood haunts and seeing his past life through the eyes of an adult.

When we got home, our phone was ringing. It was February 3rd, one month since we had left Sri Lanka. Luke went to answer the phone and I heard him shout excitedly.

"Yes, yes it is Luke." I could tell by the way he was grinning that it was Dammika. He quickly handed the phone over to me.

"Hello Tracey Lee, thank you for writing to me. I could not believe it when your letter came," he said.

I could tell he was smiling from ear to ear by the speed in which he was talking and his English was very clear. It was as though a long lost friend had found us. We had only known Dammika for five or six days but the connection we had was very strong. Before the tsunami, he was just the friendly owner of our guest house, but because of a natural disaster he had become our friend. I have never been with someone during their last precious moments with their father but I had been with Dammika when he spent those sad moments with his. I will never forget the old man being prepared for his grave.

"How are you Dammika?" I asked.

"I am not so good. After the tsunami we have had no help. Our government has done nothing," he said, sadly.

"What about all the money that has been raised worldwide, it's about thirty six million pounds," I said.

"We have seen none of it, not even the army has come to help us clean up," he told me.

"You mean it still looks the same as when we left with all the debris everywhere?" I asked.

"Yes Tracey Lee. It is a mess. Nobody help us. I am so angry with our government, they are very bad.

Now we have no tourists coming to Sri Lanka. They are scared of tsunami and we have nothing, no money to build our houses again."

I felt incredibly sad that the Sri Lankan people had been let down in this way. I had seen on television that Thailand was back up and running. They had already built new bars and apartments. In Sri Lanka it was still completely devastated. Five weeks on and nothing had changed. People across the world had donated their wages or organised fundraising events to help the zones that had been worst hit, but those in the affected areas had received none of the aid and relief that had been so generously given. Something like thirty three million pounds had been raised by the general public worldwide. Many people were too traumatised to be of any help. They were grieving and didn't dare to venture back to the village. They were relying on the help of relief workers to sift their way through the debris and start the clean-up operation.

"We owe you money Dammika, that will be a start," I said. I knew it wouldn't be enough but it would be of some help.

"Thank you Tracey Lee," said Dammika.

"We need your bank account, could you write to us with your details?"

"Yes I can," he said and we ended our call.

For five years I have organised a summer party for staff at the zoo and to raise money for various projects. I remembered that we had five hundred pounds left, so set about talking to the other party organisers. My hope was that we could give the money to Dammika to help him start rebuilding his life. I knew this would never replace the family he had lost but it might help him stand proud again. There was absolutely no hesitation from the rest of the zoo staff. They were all happy to help in this way.

27 – ST PAUL'S CATHEDRAL

Luke had heard there was going to be a memorial day at St Paul's Cathedral on Wednesday 11th May in memory of all those who lost their lives in the tsunami. We searched the internet for more information.

I scribbled down a contact number and rang it straight away. The person I spoke to told me in no uncertain terms that we would not be allowed to go. I was bitterly disappointed. She told me it was a service for the bereaved and the relief workers who had gone out to Asia after the tsunami to help bury the dead. This raised my hackles and I explained that we had been there and helped before any emergency teams arrived.

This wasn't good enough, I was curtly informed. We would not be getting an invite. I put the phone down and cried. How could somebody so far removed from the situation decide whether we were worthy of an invite? But the decision was made. We felt very sad but there was nothing we could do.

On the day of the service I went to work and pushed it to the back of my mind. I was cleaning out the hippos when a colleague of mine gave me a message to call Luke. I went to the mess room.

"Hi Luke, What's the matter?" I asked, as it is rare for him to call me at work.

"I really have an urge to go down to St Paul's and just listen to the service outside. There should be speakers set up. Do you think you can get a half day?" he said.

"I'll go and ask Malcolm," I said, and told him I'd call him back.

Malcolm, my curator, let me have a half day and leave at midday. So I rushed home to shower before travelling to Westminster. Luke met me off the bus and we had ten minutes before the service started so hurried round to the front of the Cathedral. The deep booming of the bells bought a lump to my throat and that familiar feeling of warm salty tears filled my eyes. There were many people standing around dressed in black but no speakers or screens. I watched politicians in their smart suits arrive and climb the steps of the Cathedral, one after the other.

The Queen and Prince Philip arrived and I was surprised at how much older they both looked. As soon as they had gone inside the giant doors were closed. St Paul's Cathedral has been the spiritual focus for the nation, where people and events of overwhelming importance to the country have been celebrated, mourned and commemorated since the first service took place in 1697.

We approached security to ask if we could go in but they said we needed a wristband. Disappointed, we left and walked down a narrow cobbled street. We both felt very upset. All we had wanted was to be part of the service, to pay our respects and remember the deceased. We stopped for a couple of drinks in a bar and then walked past a beautiful old pub with curved doors. It reminded me of the Old Curiosity Shop.

"I'm just going to have a peep in there, it looks lovely," I said to Luke.

I opened the door and a ray of sunlight hit a large figure standing in the corner with a pint of bitter against his tummy. He reminded me of Friar Tuck except that his robe was black. My heart leapt for joy I ran over to Luke.

"Quick we have to go in there now, there is man in there from the Cathedral," I said, excitedly.

"How do you know he's from there?" said Luke.

"I just do. He's wearing a robe. He might be able to help get us in."

Luke rolled his eyes and smiled. I grabbed his hand and dragged him towards the door of the pub. I tried to look casual as I walked past Friar Tuck. I noticed he had a folder under his arm and thought I could see the letters "Tsu…" but his robe obscured the rest as he clutched it under his arm.

The landlady and landlord were real cockney characters with big personalities. They bounced jokes backwards and forwards to one another. All the regular punters propped up the bar, laughing at their banter. I kept one eye on Friar Tuck while sipping my wine. The landlady came over to collect our empty glasses and I seized the opportunity to get chatting with her about the service over the road. I asked her if the man in the robe was from St Paul's and she said he was he was the Reverend Richard. I explained our situation and asked if she thought he would mind if I spoke to him. She said he wouldn't, so I just needed to choose my moment.

As I chatted to Luke, I felt a tap on my shoulder and there was the Reverend Richard looming over me. I was delighted. The landlady winked at me and I realised she had sorted this out. I winked back at her. He had small round glasses perched on the bridge of his nose, a chubby face with rosy cheeks, and an incredibly deep voice.

I explained that we hadn't been allowed to attend the service and wondered if he had any suggestions. He pulled from under his arm the service of remembrance for the tsunami. I was right after all. He told us that there were fifty seats that were empty because some people hadn't turned up or couldn't face coming. By now, the service was over, he said, but the Cathedral would remain open until 7.00pm as a quiet space for reflection and prayer. He instructed us to take the order of service from him and to tell the security guards that he had said we were to be allowed in. We thanked him and the landlady and hurried back.

We climbed the steps where the Queen had earlier walked and approached the monstrous doors guarded by the same security guards we had spoken to earlier. They held their arms out and said "Wristbands only."

I showed them the order of service and said, "The Reverend Richard has given us permission to go into the Cathedral."

They looked at one another doubtfully but then one took the decision to let us in.

"Thank you very much," I said, as they pushed the doors open for us.

I had been here on a college trip but had forgotten the incredible beauty and size of St Paul's. It took my breath away. The beautiful Baroque architecture made me feel very insignificant. The floor was covered in rose petals, coloured red, yellow and orange. Three hundred thousand petals had been released from the roof, in memory of those who had lost their lives in the tsunami, and had created a beautiful carpet.

We slowly walked down the aisle, treading gently on the petals. I bent down and collected one of each colour to press and keep. I took in the calm atmosphere. There was no hysteria or screaming, just peace. There were people in wheelchairs and some still had legs and arms in plaster five months on from the tsunami. I wondered what they had been through, the fear they must face daily, and how were they coping. I was not injured and was still scared to death of any sudden noise and of water. These memories would be with me for life. The injured, the panic and fear, people covered in blood, stained bandages, the crying and the frantic searching for loved ones, still missing. I stood in silence overwhelmed by the vast space. All around were the most magnificent mosaics and stained glass windows. I am not religious but always feel humbled by churches and cathedrals.

In the centre of St Paul's were twelve large alter candles. Each one had a country's name carved on it: India, Indonesia, Sri Lanka, Thailand, Bangladesh, Burma, Kenya, Malaysia, the Maldives, the Seychelles, Somalia, and Tanzania. The candles flickered gently. We lit a candle each from the Sri Lankan one and stood in silence remembering that day. I noticed Luke had tears rolling down his face, so I held his hand and cried too. We sat down and said a prayer for the victims. Both of us felt a real sense of peace from being able to pay our respects in St Paul's where many of the bereaved families had sat together earlier.

28 – COMING TO TERMS WITH A DISASTER

We are still coming to terms with what we witnessed and survived. It has taken a long time and been a long journey. Life goes on and we are all getting on with things. Whatever life throws my way, I know I will deal with it, however hard, for I have been given a second chance.

Five years to the day of the tsunami at 5.45pm on Boxing Day 2009, after six and a half hours of labour, Luke and I lost our beautiful baby boy. This was another traumatic blow but as I lay in the Whittington Hospital in North London that cold winter night my thoughts drifted back to that awful day back in 2004. I remembered Baby Harry and his poor mum. To have given birth to him, to get to know him, to love him, and then to lose him, so tragically, I gained some strength thinking about that stranger's experience. I now had a better understanding of what it felt like to be a mum. We were lucky to be able to have a funeral for our baby organised by the hospital. I can't comprehend how the families that lost their babies and children coped, having to fly back home with their little bodies.

You are never alone, somebody, somewhere has always been through what you have or worse. In many ways, my life experiences have made me stronger and able to cope with whatever cards I am dealt. I realise that at any moment everything we know and take for granted can be taken away in seconds.

When Yorkshire was flooded I panicked, thinking that the same would happen in London. The images on the news of people who had lost their homes, water everywhere, the chaos and devastation that the floods had left seemed all too familiar. Luke was away with work one night and torrential rain storms hit London. I watched through the window convinced that the Thames barriers would burst. My heart was thumping as I called Luke and asked him if I should get the cats and drive up to Muswell Hill which is the highest place near to us. He was kind and calmed me down.

Since the tsunami, there have been floods in Mumbai and Bangladesh. I watched with sadness as people died again. More recently, I watched the Haitian Earthquake. At least 200,000 people are believed to have died there.

I occasionally still have nightmares about giant waves, about panicking and running. Every now and again the sound of children screaming whilst playing at the zoo haunts me. There is a particular high pitch they hit that makes me shudder. It reminds me of people screaming for their lives. The sound transports me back to that time.

The people of Sri Lanka had to rebuild their shattered lives and start again. Many continue to live by the sea with no reassurance that this won't happen again. For those who lost their families, their homes and their livelihoods, the mental and emotional scars will take years to heal. Many of the survivors have to live with the memories of seeing loved ones and others swept away by the sea. Children were orphaned, adults widowed and hundreds of thousands died. In these devastated communities, many of those who lost their lives were never found. People have no grave to grieve beside. Because of the scale of the tragedy, the identification process was slow and painful adding to the survivors' anguish.

Throughout Asia, people believe that ghosts are the souls of people who have suffered a violent death. They are extremely fearful of ghosts and this in itself poses a big problem when pondering the horror and brutality of the tsunamis that created havoc in the region. This doesn't help the natural healing process. They believe that ghosts are still wandering the beaches.

People are terrified of returning to the beaches or living close to the sea. There are stories that haunt and frighten the locals. Tales of people hearing voices on the beach, crying, a woman calling all night from the beach, "Help me, please help me." There are accounts of a foreign ghost walking along the shoreline at night calling for her child. But the beaches are empty, there is nobody there.

These ghost stories frighten people so much that they are scared to go out after nightfall. Buddhists believe that when you die your spirit spends time as a conscious ghost seeking re-birth. Monks traditionally chant special prayers urging dead spirits to stop wandering the places where they died, to detach themselves from loved ones, so that the living can enjoy peace and the dead be re-born.

Hundreds of monks went to the beaches to pray for the dead, night after night, hoping to comfort the locals and help them adjust to life after the tsunami.

An example of how traumatised people are in Sri Lanka was bought to light only a few weeks after that awful day. There was a tsunami scare in a village called Weligama. A schoolchild had been killed in a traffic accident and on hearing the news the distraught mother ran out of her house. She ran down the beach screaming and crying. Bystanders ran after her onto the main road. More and more people joined the run spreading a wave of panic and fear through the village. Everybody was screaming and crying thinking there was a tsunami as they ran for their lives.

Their lives are shattered but I know from being with them that Sri Lankans are very resilient. Their wounds will slowly heal and they will smile once more, but it will take a long time. One thing is for sure: their experiences will be passed on for many generations to come. Tsunamis have happened before, all over the world, but we remain complacent. We have lost touch with Mother Nature and are unable to read her signs and warnings. We are now better educated about tsunamis, but at a huge cost.

We should also look closely at what we are doing to our amazing planet. The delicate balance of bio-diversity is being torn apart. We are damaging our eco-systems and natural defences, polluting our beautiful oceans, destroying animal habitats, making species extinct, chopping down and burning forests, jungles and woodlands, emptying lakes and rivers and poisoning the atmosphere.

The destruction of the mangrove swamps has proven to be detrimental to the areas that were hit by the tsunami. Their natural sea defences were removed. Educating countries about the natural world would be beneficial to both them and the planet we share. We all need to work together.

29 – RETURN TO SRI LANKA

21:12:12, 11.11am, came and went with no disaster, the Mayan prophecy that the world would end passed us by. I kind of believe anything is possible these days. I rang Luke at work at 11.12am

"We survived," I whispered.

"Good, means we are still off to Sri Lanka in six days," he said, with an exasperated tone, and hung up.

My heart sank as I sat there and wondered how I had agreed over a bottle of Chenin Blanc in The Dairy pub in Stroud Green to return to Sri Lanka on the 27th December 2012, it seemed like a good idea whilst clouded in wine, but now I wasn't so sure. Luke had persuaded me it was time to face my demons.

I knew that having to work in the elephant paddock for the past eleven years had been tough but had made me deal with the awful day of Jim's death. I knew that revisiting the scene of the tsunami would help me to have closure but I felt totally petrified and didn't want to go back.

27th December, 2012, 18.00 hours we are at an altitude of 35,000 feet, heading back, the tears roll off my face and onto my chest. I should feel lucky to have three weeks in the sun post Crimbo but I don't. Eight years and one day since the tsunami, and four years and one day since the Whittington hospital. So much has happened, time has passed, and still I cry. I am bursting with emotions that are familiar but strange as well.

There is slight turbulence which adds to my emotional roller coaster, messing up my equilibrium. Luke sits beside me trying to turn his TV screen on, I look out of the window to hide my sadness and gaze at the wing. It is pitch black outside as the night sky wraps its cloak around this metal bird, my ears are blocked, and I clutch my book by Alan Carr, *Enjoy Flying*, wishing that I had read it before the flight, but the Christmas festivities had put pay to that.

I must be grateful. In May 2012 I lost my amazing boss Mr. John Ellis, Senior Curator of Birds at London Zoo. His untimely death shattered us. I knew he would have been ecstatic to have had the opportunity to embark on this trip and see all the birds and wildlife.

I remembered as we left home for Heathrow, I had looked in the windows of the houses on our street. Christmas trees were twinkling, standing proud all dressed up in their glitz and pomp. Families were sitting around their televisions, their recycling boxes in the front gardens were crammed and spilling over with glittery wrapping paper, empty wine bottles, beer cans and cardboard boxes. I had wished I was staying with them.

We landed and I breathed a sigh of relief as the engines roared and we came to a halt. Even though the adventure was only just beginning, the first hurdle was over. It was hot and smelled familiar, the crickets were chirping and the hustle and bustle began. Luke got us a taxi to take us straight to Unawatuna. The guy looked ok, sensible, and mature, I had to trust him. I was deluded. Off we screeched for another mad journey, weaving in and out of traffic, dodging cows, dogs, bicycles, buses, tuk tuks, people, the fumes and that bloody blaring on their horns, gripping the seat and praying not to crash. Then onto the new southern highway which was faster but empty. The humidity was broken by the open window as the car sped along. I watched the Sri Lankan country side unfold in front of me. It was weird to see bright blue skies and wear my sunglasses when twelve hours ago it had been grey and cold.

I was full of anticipation and fear not knowing what to expect or how I would feel. I was thinking, thinking, thinking. Luke was fast asleep beside me. I watched the countryside go by. The water buffalos, with their loyal little egrets beside them, were lying in mud wallows, while kingfishers and bee eaters sat on the telephone wires.

We arrived safely in Unawatuna and pulled up at The Village Inn; the same sign was hanging off a new concrete post. It had the same bashed up edges from the tsunami. Nobody would know what those dents were unless you had been there, I shuddered.

Carefree travellers in brightly coloured Sri Lankan garments ambled along, dogs were yapping and barking, strutting around proudly, oblivious to their lack of hair, covered in scars and fleas. I stroked a ginger one with a sad face and an exposed rib cage; her huge swollen teats were nearly touching the floor. She looked at me with deep sad eyes and wagged her tail as if it might fall off. My heart melted. Poor little thing, Luke raised his eyebrows at me knowing full well what I was thinking. I wanted to take her home. I wondered if I might spot Chocolate in amongst these dogs but he was nowhere to be seen.

We walked down the dirt track and the humidity was a shock after coming from winter in the UK. The familiar wrought iron gates still stood at the front of The Village Inn and there was Dammika's wife. They were expecting us and she ran to get him. He appeared with a happy, welcoming smile. We were all delighted to see one another and I bit my lip so as not to cry. He had reserved room 10 for us, our room, our balcony and we all climbed up the concrete staircase together. The steps were still painted rusty red, big red ants still formed orderly lines as I stepped over them. The emotions I felt were the opposite of those which I had anticipated, I felt totally calm and safe, as if catching up with a long lost friend. It was all as I had remembered; our bed, our mirror on the bathroom wall, the fan and mosquito net, our wardrobe and the foot of the bed where on Christmas night 2004 my guardian angels had visited me.

It was eight years and one day since we had last been here. The room felt serene, not hectic or traumatic. We all stood there saying nothing. I looked over the balcony and remembered that day but not with the fear I had imagined, just sadness and a feeling of calm washed over me. I looked across to the balcony where I had seen Baby Harry being carried by his mum and dad it seemed like yesterday as if I could reach across and touch them. I felt a pang of utter disbelief, like it had all been some awful dream or film I had watched.

The stream to the left of the balcony was as it was before the tsunami, meandering through the coconut and mango trees, turquoise jade in colour, with a huge monitor lizard swimming along. I smiled and wondered if it was the same one that used to sit on the bank and had survived? There was an abundance of wildlife; sun birds fluttered over the flowers drinking their sweet nectar, flycatchers were darting about, their long whites tails leaving swirls in the memory as they flew past, shocking green bee eaters, kingfishers, woodpeckers chilling in the trees, flocks of butterflies chasing one another around and purple-faced langurs sat chewing leaves in the trees as if nothing had ever happened. I watched the animals and caught Luke watching me. We smiled at one another and said nothing.

We gave Dammika presents for his son who was now nine years old and to our surprise he bought his little sister up to the balcony. She was four years old and as cute as can be.

We didn't talk about 'that day', we just understood.

It was time for reflection. I sat on the balcony in the chair that Tim, the man from Guernsey with the torn muscle, had sat in and plopped my feet in a bowl of cold water as I had the last time we had arrived whilst Luke showered. It was hard to imagine this balcony on that day with the survivors and the injured, the fear and chaos. I tried to recall every detail.

I realised that you could no longer see through the coconut trees out across the fields as we had on that day. The jungle had regrown. The tsunami had flattened it all, exposing the land beyond. I picked up the visitors' book. There was nothing written from that day or the following year, 2005. There had been no visitors. When the comments did start in 2006 each visitor wrote about the tsunami and how Dammika told them what had happened that morning in 2004. I contemplated whether I should fill in the gaps for visitors to read and decided to do just that. I wrote my account of the tsunami and how we had returned to see Dammika and stay at The Village Inn.

I jumped out of my skin as an ear splitting clap of thunder boomed through the skies and vibrated through my feet in the bowl. I jumped up as the heavens opened and torrential monsoon rain like I had never seen before began to fall. I was shaking; every nerve in my body was alert. Flashes of lightning and thunder were terrifying in this situation, here on this balcony.

Dammika looked up from his house down below and smiled at me as if to reassure me it was ok, the water was over his ankles. I wanted to go home. I called Luke and he came out of the shower and we watched as the stream turned an orange muddy colour and started flowing faster and deeper and the ground became flooded. It stopped about thirty minutes later and thankfully got no worse.

Dammika came up and told me that he had been watching the news and was concerned that they had been having red and yellow monsoon rain in the north east of the country. This did not help to ease my nerves. Poor Dammika, he lives with this fear every day watching the news and wondering about the weather. He just shrugged his shoulders and said that this wasn't normal for this time of year.

The rain stopped, so we decided to walk to the beach. We passed the stream where I had seen Berry, my rhino friend, washing her clothes. Luke had prepared me that the seafront I had known no longer existed. As we approached I could see the waves and felt unnerved as we turned the corner. There was no beach; the sea came right up to the newly built restaurants. I was shocked. The tree that we used to sit beneath every day on the beach at the Hot Rock bar stood desolate and dead on the edge of a new restaurant and it was hard to imagine how it had been before the tsunami washed the beach away.

That evening we had a traditional Sri Lankan curry at the Hot Rock restaurant and spoke to the female owner. Half of her wall was missing in the restaurant and she explained that after the tsunami they had rebuilt next to the sea but without waiting for permission from the authorities. Then government thugs had arrived with diggers a couple of years ago and started smashing the walls down. The areas had been full of diners, but they had no care that they might injure people. As I looked along this row of bars and restaurants next to the sea, I noticed that they all had damaged walls and roofs. The Sri Lankans have had to continue working in these dangerous buildings to make a living. She told us how she had survived the tsunami but her mother and sister had not. Her eyes filled with tears and I held her hand.

That night I lay in bed listening to the fan swirling the hot air around the room and Luke snoring. I kept my eyes tightly shut in case I saw anything again. I had a restless night. The morning came and sounds of the jungle chorus filled the air. We had breakfast cooked by Dammika, two fried eggs, toast, marmalade and a big pot of tea each, and sat in the garden in the shade as the sunshine poured through the leaves. I had one ear listening for a ferocious roar. I decided I wanted to go and see The Rock and Luke agreed to come with me. I was quietly confident that I was over the tsunami and felt a real sense of achievement.

We showered and set off. It was only a short walk. I had thought it was much further away but of course the last time I had walked here was through water and over debris and I had no sense of direction. As we walked up the path to The Rock I felt my chest tighten and panic surge through my veins, my breathing quickened. It was the same, every detail, as I had remembered it: The balconies, the table where Stuart, had sat in his bandages, the well without its bouncer, the room where I helped with the bodies and the line of chairs where the bereaved and injured had sat silently with such dignity waiting for their turn in the helicopter. I held Luke's hand. In my mind I could see the pretty little Dutch girl's body being carried to her mum, and the balcony where Sunil and his wife had lain with their dead boy. My stomach knotted and I started to cry behind my sunglasses. I was overwhelmed with sadness. As a lady came out of the kitchen area and smiled at us, I realised I was standing where I had placed the dogs' water bowls that night. A deep sob left the pit of my stomach and the grief flooded my body.

"Let's go Luke," I said, and he nodded.

"I have one last place I want to go today, then that's enough until tomorrow," I said.

"Ok. Where?" he asked

"To the hill where I tended to the woman on the bench," I replied.

"Of course," said Luke, putting his arm around my shoulder and guiding me away from The Rock.

We passed the area where the mass grave had been dug. It was covered in gigantic boulders. We stood silently in thought, holding hands, reflecting on the whole unbelievable experience. We carried on walking to the foot of the hill. I remembered the dead bodies with banana leaves covering their faces, the ground, blood-stained from their injuries, the mud, fishes flapping around and the fences with their trapped victims, as if it was yesterday.

I looked up the hill and knew exactly where she had lain. We stopped. I didn't want to go any further. I blew a kiss and we turned and walked away. I picked up my pace, wanting to get back to the safety of The Village Inn a quickly as possible.

On the way back, we saw Peter, the Sri Lankan man we had tried to help get into to his house. He didn't recognise us, so we didn't say anything. I didn't want to upset him with our memories. He was chatting with friends and looked OK.

I did however still want to see Thalik and Sunil. Luke told me that Sunil might not remember us but, regardless, I wanted to try. We walked to where Sunil's café and bar had been and found a very swish place had been built in its place. It opened up into lovely grounds with water features and beautiful plants. We ordered a beer and a gin and tonic. One of the waiters approached me:

"Miss…. I know you from Christmas night 2004, before tsunami, we spent the night drinking, dancing and playing music, over there," he pointed excitedly, desperate for me to remember where we had sat.

"Yes, we did," I agreed. I thought I recognised his face and we hugged and laughed. He seemed thrilled and was telling all the waiters who we were, nodding and smiling at us. He told us that Sunil was away shopping in Colombo and would be back the next day and we agreed that we would return then. He pointed to a woman with red hair who was busy serving tables and said that she was Sunil's new wife. I approached her and explained our story and asked if she thought we should come back or whether it was best not too. She smiled and told us to pop by.

The next day we went back, ordered drinks, and sat down amongst the beautiful plants. When Sunil walked over to us I did not recognise him at all and, at first, he didn't appear to know who we were either. His long, curly hair was now sharply cut and flecked with grey. He no longer dressed like a hippy but wore smart shorts, an ironed shirt and flip flops rather than bare feet. We started chatting and he told us how his marriage to Helga, who had been pregnant at the time of the tsunami, had ended. She had returned to Germany. He had been there only once to meet his daughter, now eight years old. He was happily married to Helen who, coincidentally, was also

German.

I asked Sunil if he still had his dog, Chocolate, and he looked at me, surprised that I would remember such a thing. He raised his eyebrows, bemused, and said that he hadn't seen him for six months; he had gone missing and he presumed he was dead.

We finished our drinks and said our goodbyes to Sunil. He seemed pleased to have chatted with us. The waiter came and shook our hands and Sunil's wife winked at me with an approving smile. He obviously thrown his life and soul into his business and it had paid off. On our way out, in the reception, I noticed two pictures hanging side by side – one of his beautiful son and the other of his mother, who he had also lost in the tsunami. I looked at them and remembered his son that Christmas night, laughing and smiling.

We walked out into the night and I was pleased that I had been given this opportunity to talk with Sunil. We were lost in our own thoughts ambling along the dusty, warm road watching the fire flies sparkling emerald green and bright red against the stars.

I thought about the people I had been with that day at the zoo when Jim was killed and knew that although we had all been joined together during that horrific and intimate time I would never be able to pick out their faces in a line up, I couldn't even picture the paramedics who I had talked to, because shock and trauma overrides all memory.

We left Unawatuna the next day. It was New Year's Day, 2013. We said goodbye to Dammika and his family stood and waved us off until we were out of sight. We had one last place to go: Zimmer Rest. As we walked up the dusty drive, we could see that the verandah was full of visitors sitting around having breakfast. It was still framed with tropical vegetation and I remembered us all opening our Christmas presents here, hung over, all laughing at the cat book that I had bought Luke.

The painting of the female tea pickers still hung on the wall. We plonked our heavy bags down and entered the foyer. The walls were plastered with Thalik's wooden Sri Lankan masks and there in the middle of his counter was the Japanese Good Luck Cat that Fran had given him before the tsunami. Again it was as if it was yesterday. I half expected to see Pat and Fran to be sitting on the balcony.

We asked if Thalik was around and were disappointed to learn that he was in Kandy.

We had decided to leave the sea and head to the National Parks of Bundala and Yala to go on safari. We didn't want to only remember this wonderful country with horror. Luke flagged down a local bus from the side of the road and as we started to climb on the driver was shouting at us:

"Quickly, Quickly!"

As we staggered on with our heavy bags, he started to drive off. I screamed as he floored the accelerator. He was soon speeding at 70mph. Loud Sri Lankan music was booming out of the speakers. It was crowded so we were standing with our bags, hanging on for dear life, being flung from side to side, on top of people that were sitting down. The driver had one hand on the wheel; the other held his mobile to his ear. Every so often, he would let go of the wheel to blare on his horn. As he approached bends he accelerated and swerved onto the opposite side of the road, blind to what was oncoming – Lorries, buses, people, cows, dogs, bikes, tuk tuks. It was terrifying. I seriously thought we would be killed in an accident.

On one bend a white car came head on at us and screeched off the road. It probably crashed, we will never know. Eventually we got two seats and, still shaking, I sat down as the bus skidded from side to side, screeching, missing head on collisions with inches to spare. I looked out of the window and tried to calm my nerves. I was fuming at having put my life in this idiot's hands. Luke sat silently beside me. After a while and for no apparent reason he slowed down, so we had time to catch our breath. The local people were all still looking at me but I didn't care.

All along this coastal route from Unawatuna to Tangalle there were ruins from the tsunami, ghostly foundations where homes had once stood, the odd bit of wall that had withstood the wave covered in a kind of black mould. The sea was on the other side of the road and I felt uneasy, trapped in this bus. New houses had been built next to the ruins. On some of the foundations were gravestones covered in weeds and black mould. Sometimes there were twelve or more or one stood alone. I imagined who had lived there. Whole families and communities had been wiped out.

The Sri Lankans have rebuilt their lives as best they can. However, every person you meet wants to talk about the tsunami. They all have a story of loss, whether it's family, home, business or everything. Behind their kind smiles is a haunted look. I lost nothing but am still traumatised by this catastrophic event and cannot comprehend what these people have had to go through. I am full of admiration for them and our return to Sri Lanka was a humbling experience.

On 13th January 2013 we head back to London. Finally, I feel as though I have some closure. I have faced my demons. My book has taken over eight years to write and Sri Lanka has been in my thoughts, day in, day out, since 26th December 2004. Although I will never forget what happened it is time to get on with my life and enjoy every minute that I have left.

PHOTOS BELOW FROM RETURN TRIP

Return to Sri Lanka – Christmas 2013

From the balcony that saved our lives!

ROCK
House
GUEST HOUSE
213/A Yaddehimulla Rd,
Unawatuna

ABOUT THE AUTHOR

Tracey lives in Stroud Green, North London with her partner Luke. Their cats Frank and Mindy and their koi carp. She studied at Bournville School of Art in Birmingham. She is the Team Leader of Mammals South at the Zoological Society of London and has worked there for 25 years. During this time she has been lucky enough to work with some of the planet's most amazing creatures from giant pandas and lowland gorillas, to pygmy hippos, black rhinos and Sumatran tigers.

Tracey and Luke are seasoned travellers and have enjoyed travelling throughout Asia over the years.

With many sad and wonderful life experiences she wrote her memoirs over the past eight years from her home after work.

Tracey with Nadia her Bactrian camel